The Shakespeare Complex

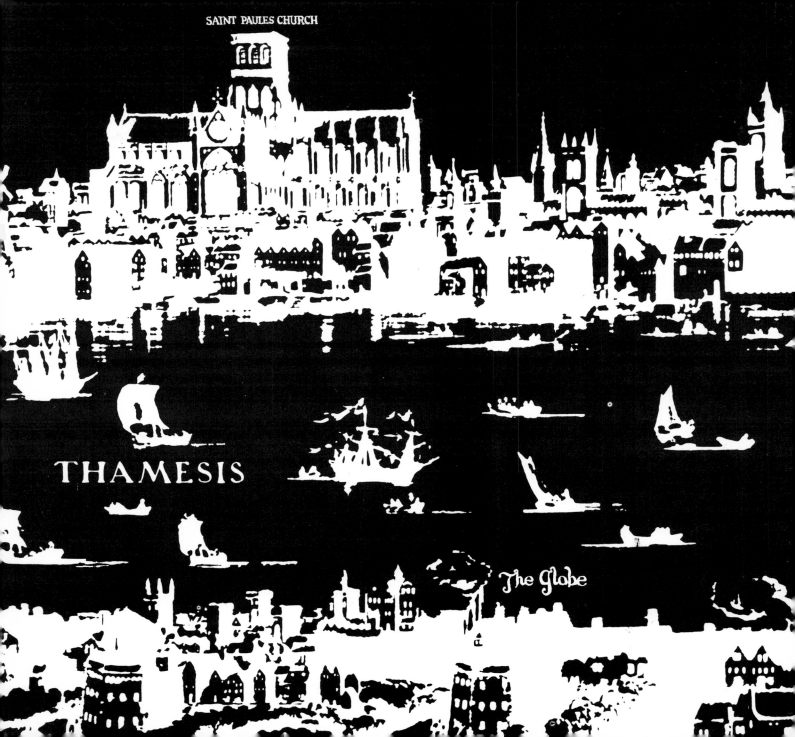

The Shakespeare Complex

*A guide to summer
festivals and year-round repertory
in North America*

by Glen Loney and Patricia MacKay

DRAMA BOOK SPECIALISTS (PUBLISHERS) *New York*

Library of Congress Cataloging in Publication Data
MacKay, Patricia.
        The Shakespeare complex: a guide to summer festivals and year round repertory.

        1. Shakespeare, William, 1564–1616—Stage history—1950   2. Theater—United States. 3. Theater—Canada. I. Loney, Glenn Meredith, 1928–   joint author. II. Title
PR3100.M3   792'.0973   75-15594
ISBN 0-910482-61-6
ISBN 0-910482-62-4

DESIGN BY BETTY BINNS

ACKNOWLEDGEMENTS

Two groups must be thanked for the existence of this book: First, Rodale Press's *Theatre Crafts* magazine, Marshall Ackerman, publisher and C. Ray Smith, former editor. It was for the March/April 1973 issue of *Theatre Crafts* that research on Shakespeare festivals in the United States and Canada was first initiated.

Second, the festivals themselves—for the generous support, encouragement, and assistance which we received from festival artistic directors, designers, publicists, and photographers.

Contents

Shakespeare Tours

Shakespeare Celebrations

The Shakespeare Complex

Forms
and
Facets

More than productions; a state of mind

The Oregon Shakespearean Festival draws visitors from across the nation to the town of Ashland, where each night of the summer season, the company performs outdoors on a recreation of an Elizabethan stage.

The Shakespeare Complex is two things. First and most visibly, it is a collection of theatre organizations, some repertory companies, and summer festivals, as well as a number of colleges and universities that are devoting all, or part, of their production work to the plays of William Shakespeare. And, secondly, The Shakespeare Complex is a state of mind.

Individually, the members of The Shakespeare Complex are varied. They might be groups that started life as summer projects—such as the two Stratfords—one in Ontario and one in Connecticut. Their success has been such that over the years the acting ensembles have developed into strong, respected companies, producing plays from a wide range of periods and in a wide range of styles. Each group has outgrown its reliance on the works of the Bard, and each has undertaken longer seasons.

The Stratford Connecticut Shakespeare group concentrates its production season in the summer. But demand for student performance has found the theatre opening its doors in the late spring. And now, they are considering reinstituting a fall or winter touring season. Frequently, the summer season extends to a fall Broadway run for a particularly successful play. Most recently their production of *Cat on a Hot Tin Roof* moved to New York. The Canadian Festival has expanded into almost 10 months of play production, in three theatres, as well as tours both in Canada and abroad. These two Stratfords began life as Shakespeare Festivals, and have moved on to less restricting self-definitions. In Ontario, the word "Shakespeare" has been dropped to make that group The Stratford Festival of Canada. In Connecticut, the word "Festival" has been dropped, making that group The American Shakespeare Theatre. Among the contemporary Shakespeare producing organizations, there is some contention about the exact usage of the term "festival." Some groups refuse to include the phrase in their name, claiming that it indicates either a short season, or the inclusion of special events, or big-name, guest actors and directors. Other groups are not so particular.

But these two prestigious theatrical groups are not alone in their success. Perhaps the most spectacular rise from small, summer, Shakespeare production to full-blown year-round repertory theatre operation (on nine different stages) has been that of the New York Shakespeare Festival Theatre, under Joseph Papp. Nor should a somewhat quieter operation in California be overlooked: the San Diego National Shakespeare Festival also began as a strictly summer operation, but is now a year-round producing organization utilizing two unusual theatre spaces. The Oregon Shakespearean Festival has expanded into a spring season and the Globe of the Great Southwest (in Odessa, Texas) has recently begun producing year-round.

Also included in the Shakespeare Complex are new repertory companies such as The Rochester Shakespeare Theatre. While concentrating on producing the Bard's works, this group, until its recent demise, was also using his name as a drawing card for their other plays. It is a means of creating instant acceptance and status in a community. The Emeryville Shakespeare Company has recently surfaced in Berkeley, California. Conversely, The Folger Theatre Group which makes its home in a reconstructed Elizabethan theatre located in one of the world's bastions of Shakespeare scholarship—The Folger Library—does not use Shakespeare as a drawing card. They do produce a Shakespeare play usually in honor of his birthday.

Universities and colleges are also part of the Complex. Among them are Hofstra University on Long Island and Columbia College in Georgia. Both these schools have honored Shakespeare with attempts to reconstruct the Globe Theatre. These imaginative evocations of Elizabethan theatre life have become the centerpiece of annual Shakespeare productions. At the Universities of Vermont and Colorado, there are annual summer Shakespeare Festivals—but no Globe Theatre. Communities, too, sponsor Shakespeare Festivals—with varying degrees of professionalism. Among them are Monmouth (Maine), Los Angeles, Anniston (Alabama), Lakewood (Ohio), Washington, D. C., Louisville, and *two* New Jersey towns: Madison and Woodbridge.

In addition, the roundup of groups concerning themselves with Shakespeare production includes several companies that have no permanent theatre home. The National Shakespeare Company tours productions of many classic plays, including works by the Bard, to theatres and schools throughout the country. The Southeastern Shakespeare Company takes excerpts to high schools and colleges in North Carolina and the surrounding territories. San Francisco's New Shakespeare Company takes its productions into most regions of the nation.

In a series of gestures that seems to combine an awareness of America's reverence for things Shakespearean as well as things British, the Royal Shakespeare Company and the National Theatre have made visits to the United States in the past few years. The RSC's celebrated and controversial Peter Brook production of *A Midsummer Night's Dream* was performed during two tours in widely scattered centers. Not to be outdone, the National exported its all-male *As You Like It* to the New World. The RSC and the Brook *Dream* were so well received at the Brooklyn Academy of Music that its guiding genius, Harvey Lichtenstein, decided to launch 1974 with a British Theatre Season. With great success, he brought over the Royal Shakespeare, the Actors Company, and the Young Vic. In 1975, the RSC staged a return visit. Both seasons were the focal point of seminars at Brooklyn College and New York University.

The complex of Shakespeare festivals is active and impressive. Every effort has been made to discover and document Shakespeare festivals in the United States and Canada, but this is not a cohesive group of theatres or producing organizations, and it is possible that a new regional or a community festival may have been missed. Plans for new Shakespeare festivals are almost always in the works: Hawaii is thinking about adding one to their roster of tourist attractions; and in the spring of 1975, Arts Unlimited was formed in San Antonio, Texas, to offer a season of Shakespeare in the high schools. As frequent as are the Festival births—so too are the deaths. Causes vary: the University of Kansas, which sponsored a Shakespeare Festival and Institute for two summers, in 1974, switched to festivals of American playwrights. It contemplates an irregular return to Shakespeare. More often, Festival demises can be blamed on administrative problems, poor judgment of a festival's market, and financial troubles—troubles which are even less soluble in times of widespread economic recession. Such a recent casualty was Minneapolis' Shakespeare-in-the-Streets; lack of funds forced them to cancel their 1975 season—however the producers insist they will return. The San Francisco Shakespearean Festival, currently inactive, appears to have over extended itself when it moved from its Marin County outdoor theatre to the San Francisco Palace of Fine Arts. The Rochester Shakespeare Theatre, after several seasons of exciting work, found in late 1974 that their support from within the community could not meet the costs of their season—they, too, have now closed their doors.

The Shakespeare Complex appears to be a peculiarly North American disease. For all the honor Englishmen render unto Shakespeare with stagings at Stratford-upon-Avon, in London, and at major and minor provincial repertory centers, it is the North Americans who have shown the greatest passion for

Ever increasing audiences forced some festivals, like Ashland (below), to expand their facilities by adding another theatre. At Ashland the addition of an indoor space to their theatre complex also permits them to expand the performance season into the fall and spring. Other festivals—like the Champlain Shakespeare Festival (bottom) make use of university and college theatre facilities for a summer season of Shakespeare's plays.

and industry in the production and preservation of Shakespeare. Can it be the former colonies' desire to maintain a link with the Motherland? Perhaps. The search for a historical and cultural heritage? Maybe. But, certainly, Shakespeare is, in the minds of most Americans and Canadians, equivalent to "accepted culture." He has become a cultural talisman. To admit a distaste for Shakespeare or his plays is tantamount to blasphemy.

Beyond the visible network of cities and towns, the consortium of theatres, shops, personnel and productions, the Shakespeare Complex is a state of mind. It is a state of mind which not only permits, but also seems to encourage ecstatic reverence for the Bard's words. Some might call it a fanaticism, others a dedication. Certainly, it is a very special state of mind which has encouraged the attempts at rebuilding Shakespeare's own playhouse. It has made possible the many festivals in his honor, and the Shakespeare study centers, such as the Folger Shakespeare Library in Washington, D.C. or the Huntington Library in San Marino, California. It has also produced an almost endless bibliography of magazines, special features, special academic courses and seminars, films, records, and books of Shakespeareana.

Given the large number of English departments in American colleges and universities, in addition to the drama departments, it is scarcely to be wondered that there are so many scholarly gatherings and publications devoted to analysis of Shakespeare's works, his period, and theatre conventions. Among the more important and specifically Shakespearean publications—not counting those edited in England and elsewhere abroad—are *The Shakespeare Newsletter, The Folger Library Newsletter, The Shakespeare Quarterly*—also issued by the Folger, and the annual *Shakespeare Studies,* published in Columbia, South Carolina.

Many schools and colleges have their own annual or occasional Shakespeare colloquies, seminars, and production study projects. The University of Texas at Austin turns an English course into summer study called Shakespeare at Winedale. The Kansas Shakespeare Festival was inextricably tied to a summer institute studying history, music, and manners of the period. The University of New Hampshire devoted one recent season of their summer theatre program to Shakespeare. Hofstra University and Columbus College turn a single play production into an event of history and revelry. And, the University of Michigan was the scene of celebration in 1974 when—according to their report—they became the first educational institution to complete production of the entire canon—a feat only accomplished seven other times. One of these was at Antioch College in Yellow Springs, Ohio, where director Arthur Lithgow completed the canon in 1956.

The result of such "Bardolatry" is that—whether the production is good or bad—Shakespeare brings out audiences which otherwise would not frequent live theatre. There appear to be no other playwrights with such magnetism. At present in America and Canada, there are more than two score of festivals or annual special events in honor of Shakespeare. Yet, while there is an Eugene O'Neill Center for the Performing Arts, there is no annual festival of his plays. True, there is an annual Shaw Festival in Canada, hardly his homeland. But there are no annual festivals to honor native American playwrights such as Arthur Miller, Tennessee Williams, David Belasco, Robert E. Sherwood, Maxwell Anderson, Kaufman and Hart, Philip Barry, or Neil Simon.

Only a reputation as big as Will Shakespeare's makes it possible for a culture-hungry group of townspeople to band together, found a festival, and actually expect to attract a paying audience. Considering the range and variety offered by the complete

The Stratford Festival of Canada and the New York Shakespeare Festival are most noted for the production of the work of new playwrights.

The Stratford Festival of Canada: *Inook and The Sun* by Henry Beissel *(top)*; *The Friends* by Arnold Wesker *(center)*.

The New York Shakespeare Festival: *Ti-Jean & His Brothers* by Derek Walcott *(left)*.

canon of Shakespeare's works, festival producers have a marvelous commodity to manipulate. In addition to the wide choice of plays for summer repertory—comedy, history, tragedy, comical-history, and tragical-comedy, to misquote Polonius—a number of the plays are well known to potential audiences. Some plays are even feared and/or revered from minute dissections in high school or college classes. In the 37 dramas attributed wholly or in part to Shakespeare, there are incredible riches of plot, sub-plot, character, theme, language, and spectacle. Not to mention strong incitements to sentimental sniffling, uproarious laughter, or slow-growing anger. Actors long to play the parts. Directors are dying to stage them. Audiences are fascinated. Nor should it be overlooked that the entire canon is royalty free.

Another very "American" aspect of the festivals is the sociology of the play selection. There appears to be a continuing concern that the festival plays be "relevant" to contemporary experiences. Needless to say, there are those groups that stage the Bard's work without ulterior motive, but for others *Julius Caesar* was a natural choice for the assassination-prone 1960's. *Romeo and Juliet* spoke to the generation of flower children. *The Taming of the Shrew* and *The Merchant of Venice* seem designed to prove a point for the feminist movement. In the summers of Watergate, there was a rash of escape-the-political-structure plays in the form of *As You Like It*; *Measure for Measure* makes a point about moral corruption in high places; while *Coriolanus* displays an overwhelming contempt for the People and for government by those People. Whether or not the artistic directors admit to deliberate selection, the more relevant the theme, the more value many pragmatic Americans are likely to find in the live theatre.

Reverence to the Bard is paid in nooks and crannies all over North America. There are reverent reconstructions of Elizabethan theatres, carefully detailed costuming—from medieval wimples to cross-gartered hose—and there is concern with producing the entire canon of plays—whether or not they actually merit staging. The festivals are flanked with mini-happenings: madrigal singers, hawkers of folksy wares, sellers of healthful foods. These foods range from mint teas in Boulder, Colorado, to plastic baggies of bread, fruit and nuts in New York's Central Park. In one sense, it is clear that Shakespeare has become an excuse for a picnic on the lawn at Stratford, Connecticut. In another, a scenic camping trip through the American West may have as its goal a visit to the Utah Shakespeare Festival in Cedar City—not far from Bryce and Zion National Parks. There have even been tentative explorations of Diamond Head Crater, Hawaii, as a future festival and Globe Theatre site.

Whatever the motives for attending Shakespeare festivals, Americans and Canadians are increasingly involved in the Shakespeare Complex. It has become a positive force in the life of North American Theatre. It is bringing live theatre into many communities which otherwise would never experience anything more lively than a TV special. It provides work for actors, designers, directors, and craftspeople. It has brought the work of Shakespeare to life for hundreds of thousands of Americans and Canadians who have in turn moved on to support and encourage a wider range of theatrical experiences. The complex of Shakespeare festivals—and all that they entail—shows signs of becoming a base from which a solid group of American and Canadian resident, regional theatre companies will grow. Indeed some of the most outstanding festivals already fill that bill. And, there is hope that they may even become the training ground in classical theatre that is unavailable to actors and directors in North America.

Lastly, a word needs to be said about criticism.

The individual chapters on festivals in the book are deliberately sparse in the type of appraisals in which newspaper—and other media—critics indulge. That kind of per-performance rating would only be unfair to the festivals involved in a continuing program of production and growth. In addition, many of the festivals change rapidly from season to season so that any current criticism would be invalid next year. Where there seems a stable resident company of actors, designers, and directors—as in San Diego, New York, or Stratford, Connecticut—we have indicated the now-recognizable quality of their work. In other instances, like Alabama, Dallas, or Los Angeles, the groups are too young to have yet established a coherent image. Additionally, festivals which have seemed "established" are now changing. The Colorado Shakespeare Festival has become known for its consistently good costuming. The costumer responsible, Thomas Schmunk, left at the close of the 1973 season; the 1974 season costumer stayed only one summer, and another new approach to costume-work is due for Colorado in 1975. Even the Stratford Festival of Canada is in for change: artistic director Jean Gascon departed in 1974, and Robin Phillips has replaced him.

All we can hope to do is to indicate the areas of potential criticism, the difficulties that each festival has or will come up against. We point them out by way of encouraging the festivals to devise, and for the audience to demand, solutions. It is not our intention in any way to discourage Shakespeare productions because they might not live up to any golden ideal of good theatre. Any festival that continues to bring in an audience must be doing something right. Given the limitations of their budgets, physical situations, and audience tolerance, we can only hope that each member of the Shakespeare Complex will try still harder. They have become a way of life.

Battling with the Bard

Festival standards in perspective

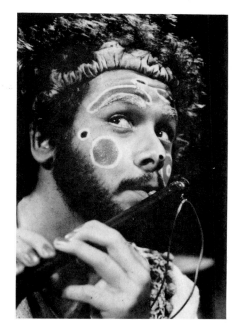

The Rochester Shakespeare Theatre: *Twelfth Night*. The company recently suspended operations after several year-round seasons.

The Shakespeare Complex and its attendant festival play productions are, at least in North America, a relatively recent phenomenon. Of course, during the 18th and 19th Centuries, there were tours and celebrated productions by great actors and actresses in works by William Shakespeare. There have also been annual productions at educational institutions, as well as repertory and limited engagements on the commercial Broadway stage. But, the concept of bringing actors and directors together for a special, unified celebration does not seem to have taken hold in this country until the mid-1930's with Angus Bowmer's Oregon Shakespearean Festival. The organization of the San Diego National Shakespeare Festival was not far behind.

In Shakespeare's own homeland, it was not until 1769 that the first festival "Jubilee at Stratford in Honor and to the Memory of Shakespeare" took place. The distinguished actor David Garrick decided to link his name with that of the Bard's forever by organizing this Jubilee.

This first of all Shakespeare festivals began in bedlam and ended in disaster. The crowds which descended on Stratford-upon-Avon—then only a sleepy provincial town—were far too large for the available accommodations. Dr. Johnson's chronicler, James Boswell, was hard put to find a bed. Runaway carriages made the streets unsafe. Garrick was so badly cut while being shaved that he was almost unable to recite the choral ode he had invented for the occasion. A 327-pound turtle, provided for the gala banquet, was not all it might have been. On the second of three days set aside for the festival, a rainstorm began, signaling other near calamities. The costly costume pageant of all Shakespeare's characters was ruined. What should have been a magnificent display of fireworks sputtered out in the dampness. The great masquerade ball, held in the riverside Rotunda, had its moments, but steadily falling

9

rain made the Avon rise so rapidly that a number of masquers had to swim back to their lodgings.

Fortunately, tales of woe from contemporary festivals seldom match Garrick's First Jubilee—although most of the current festivals are not without their difficulties. Some problems are physical, others monetary, and still others ideological. Putting together a Shakespeare festival is not easy. Audiences will find themselves facing a wide range of professional skills. Productions run from brilliant to poor, with degrees in between that include uneven acting, pedestrian directing, inappropriate and inconsequential costume or set design, or simply inattention to details. There can be such minor distractions as mis-pronounced words, or hearing a dark-haired actor describe his gray locks.

Outdoor theatres undoubtedly are the most difficult festival homes. There is a constant threat of rain. High winds can blow settings over. Street noises and low flying aircraft do their best to disrupt performances. Not even the highly professional New York Shakespeare Festival has managed to "mike" their actors so the audience will not be jolted when summer winds do blow, or when hero and heroine come together in a crushing clinch. While an audience might be tolerant of outdoor conditions, they can quickly become impatient with a small, amateur Shakespeare group performing in an awkward indoor space with inadequate lighting equipment. Such troupes often fight a losing battle with their physical surroundings.

No matter how a director chooses to interpret a Shakespeare play, some member of the audience is bound to be displeased. A rock-musical modernization might be more meaningful for young audiences, but it is not likely to receive kudos from classical production buffs. Even with the most star-studded collection of well-known actors and directors, the creation of magnificent Shakespearean productions is not automatic. The New York Shakespeare Festival, the American Shakespeare Theatre, and the Stratford Festival of Canada have all fallen on their faces more than occasionally.

Some festivals are hampered by the combined youth and inexperience of both the director and the actors. Although it is certainly a trade-off. While the youthful festival personnel may not yet have the insights to stage a meaningful interpretation of Shakespeare, they do have enthusiasm to work long and hard for little money in order to launch a new theatre venture.

Some regional festivals are finding it difficult to see their productions in critical perspective. Local reviewers have a tendency to be effusive about hometown theatre efforts. Occasionally regional critics are inexperienced with serious critical analysis. Visiting critics from national magazines and well-known newspapers tend to be kind to any regional theatre activity. That kindness, combined with local enthusiasm, creates a smoke-screen which prevents artistic directors from seeing clearly exactly where a festival's work is really solid and reputable and where it can beneficially be improved.

Spectators at various North American Shakespeare festivals might assume that the engagement of directors and designers with professional credits or the formation of an Equity company will guarantee a high professional standard of performance. But it isn't always true. Many a member of an Equity cast is less talented than the struggling apprentice who one day may have a great professional career. Frequently, the summer festival Shakespeare work is a way-station for aspiring actors and designers. In fact, there is at least one regional festival which boasts an Equity ensemble, and yet offers performances which are not much better than those turned in by graduate drama students at some of the college festivals. That does not mean, of course, that

The American Shakespeare Theatre: *The Tempest*

Equity companies are to be avoided in favor of collegiate casts.

A great deal of the blame and/or credit rests with the directors. A festival director who assembles a group of mediocre performers—with or without union cards—cannot expect much from the resultant productions. Some plays, of course, are actor-proof. But *Macbeth* is not *Charley's Aunt,* and no amount of ranting, mugging, and posing is going to fool an audience into thinking they are seeing a memorable performance of a great Shakespearean tragedy.

There are, of course, festival directors who obviously have a very real love of Shakespeare, as well as an intuitive understanding of the canon. There are others who do not. Some directors even intimate that they have no strong affinity for Shakespeare, but choose to stage his works since they seem to be unfailing audience magnets. For them, Shakespeare is an entertainment commodity which, oddly enough, is even more sure-fire than Neil Simon.

Many of the festival directing jobs are assigned to directors whose experience has been almost entirely limited to working in colleges and universities, directing casts of students for an audience composed mainly of students. Frequently, the educational theatre director does not have the overview or the technical proficiency of a more experienced director from the professional theatre. Conversely, the educational theatre director can display a tight control, interesting interpretational concepts, and an enlightened visual sense.

An inventive, inspiring director—professional or academic—together with an eager ensemble—Equity or not—is likely to generate exciting or, at the very least, intelligent productions of Shakespeare's plays. In any event, no good purpose can be served here by loudly condemning either mediocre stagings or inadequate players. Conscientious critics and increased audience awareness can, however, encourage solidly established and handsomely subsidized festivals to mend their ways. Unfortunately, many of the festivals which should strive most for a better production quality are also victims of seasonal insecurity and inadequate subsidies. Demanding that they be bold, imaginative, and excellent is probably asking too much when they are not even certain of survival. The festivals need intelligent encouragement and support—especially in the area of building operational subsidies, which in turn can help them to improve their work.

There is another danger: that critics who are too generous and considerate in their reviews will find their judgments being questioned by disappointed audiences. Or worse—inadequate directors could become smug from reading uninformed raves. The problem, then, is to maintain a positive supportive attitude without overlooking mistakes and miscarriages in staging Shakespeare.

Bringing the Bard to Life

Directors and actors rush to accept the challenge

The New Shakespeare Company: *A Midsummer Night's Dream*

Hamlet, to many of the English-speaking theatre's leading actors, has been a challenge they could not resist. In fact, for well over three hundred years they have not resisted the attractions and pitfalls of this taxing tragic role, but most of them have instead fairly leapt at opportunities to play it. Some have intrigued to create such opportunities. Women have also been fascinated by the role. The most recent to play it "in breeches" was none other than the distinguished actress Dame Judith Anderson, though she was some decades older than this ambivalent hero—if verisimilitude is any criterion in casting.

Hamlet is by no means a uniquely appealing role. At different periods in their careers, most actors and actresses working in the British or North American theatre will feel that the time has come for them to play certain major Shakespearean roles. Romeo, Hamlet, and Henry V, for instance, usually attract young actors; Juliet, Ophelia, and Portia are only a few of the youthful heroines which ingenues are eager to play. As the body ages, the emotions mature, the intellect ripens, and the performance techniques become more secure, actors and actresses are naturally anxious to play Shakespeare's more mature, more complex, more demanding heroic roles, as well as some tempting character parts such as Juliet's Nurse, Malvolio, Polonius, and Queen Margaret.

When Lord Olivier felt he was finally ready to play Othello, he found the physical and emotional strains of the role were exhausting. At the age when he first interpreted Hamlet, he had far more of the energy and stamina Othello required, but, as he has pointed out, he did not yet have enough experience as an actor or a human being to flesh out the character to its widest dimensions. This will always be a problem for performers: finding the right time in their careers—and the right place and the right production—to explore the Shakespearean roles they long to play.

In Great Britain and in Europe, there is at least the

The lure of Shakespeare draws audience to well-known and familiar plays: *King Lear* at the Utah Shakespeare Festival *(far right)*; *Romeo and Juliet* at the Folger Theatre Group *(right bottom)*; and *Love's Labour's Lost* at the Oregon Shakespearean Festival *(bottom)*. Shakespeare also draws performers to try a hand at his many roles: Eva LeGallienne and Peter Thompson in *All's Well That Ends Well* at the American Shakespeare Theatre *(right)*; and Gretchen Corbett and Richard Council in *As You Like It* at the New Jersey Shakespeare Festival *(below)*.

possibility of playing a variety of roles in the comedies, histories, and tragedies. Shakespeare has always been popular with British theatre groups, whether amateur or professional. On the continent, the Bard's plays are a staple of any reputable state or city-subsidized theatre's season.

For American and Canadian actors and actresses, however, there is not nearly as much opportunity to experiment with Shakespeare's plays, to grow and develop in skills and insights required by the themes, plots, characters, and language of the dramas. Many a young American actor will probably never get the chance to play a major role in a competent professional production.

The same sense of frustration afflicts many talented older performers. The late Robert Ryan, after winning a solid reputation as a cinema "tough guy," hazarded his fame with a Coriolanus on the New York stage in 1954. Critics, possibly suspicious of film stars, suggested that he had played the role like a gangster. While this wounded him a bit, it did not deter him from seeking other opportunities. Later, he played Antony to Katharine Hepburn's Cleopatra at the American Shakespeare Festival in Stratford, Connecticut. Some time after that, he was invited to play Othello at the Nottingham Theatre in England, back-to-back with Eugene O'Neill's father-figure in *A Long Day's Journey into Night*.

Of this experience, he said, "Each performance got better, naturally. In the first place, it is an almost total reversal of the kind of acting one does generally, the so-called realistic, slice-of-life acting. Very simply, you can't walk around with your hands in your pockets. You can't light cigarettes. You never—or almost never—sit down. In playing Shakespeare, you stand alone, with whatever resources you have. Your vocal problems are enormous. You have to sustain long melodic speeches from the beginning of a paragraph to the end, which very seldom happens in a modern play. You have to find a way to give it full poetic value and yet keep it real . . ."

As Broadway and Off-Broadway production wanes—particularly discouraging to any thoughts of Shakespeare revivals, other than those generated and occasionally musicalized by the New York Shakespeare Festival—annual festivals of the Bard's works and regional theatre repertory stagings seem the only possible outlets for passionate, if frustrated, acting talents.

The same is true for directors. Ed Sherin, who won almost instant acclaim for his production of *The Great White Hope*, followed its initial staging for the Washington, D.C., Arena Theatre with a *King Lear*. Intelligently conceived from a directorial point of view, the production was unsatisfactory. After a matinee one day, Sherin confessed to a personal disappointment with the total production, despite the brilliance of Frank Silvera's Lear. He agreed that the lack of proper training and skills had prevented some cast members from bringing the tragedy to vibrant, meaningful life. "But," he explained a bit defensively, "*Lear* is the play every director worth his salt has *got* to do. I wanted to see how I could stage it." Fortunately for Sherin, he was given another opportunity to try his hand with *King Lear*. In the summer of 1973, he staged it for Joseph Papp's Central Park fest, with James Earl Jones as Lear. Changes and developments in the Sherin vision of the drama were obvious.

Thus far, it might seem that the score or more of American and Canadian Shakespeare festivals are primarily of value because they permit actors and directors to learn their crafts and polish their skills, while releasing pressures of frustration which might otherwise drive them berserk. It is true that the festivals do provide both good training grounds and valuable emotional therapy, but, for really dedicated performers and directors, there is a lot more to the challenge than that. The main thing, of course, is to provide an enjoyable, illuminating experience for the audiences.

That means that, no matter how much a leading actor may be dying to perform *Pericles* or a famed director to stage *Timon of Athens,* a balanced festival program must be provided. A favorite formula used by astute directors is to offer two Shakespearean comedies and one tragedy. More risky is one comedy, one tragedy, and one history play. Even when a festival operation is dedicated to the goal of producing the entire canon, as has been done at Antioch College, the University of Michigan, and the Oregon Shakespearean Festival, the thirty-seven plays will almost never be staged one after another. *The Comedy of Errors* may receive three or four summer productions before *Cymbeline* is tried even once, despite dreams of completing the canon on stage. This may be a bit discouraging to the director who has his heart set on doing *Cymbeline,* but part of a director's training is to learn what has the best chance of attracting audiences.

Among the more popular of the Bard's plays, judging from directorial choices for recent festivals, are such works as *Romeo and Juliet, Hamlet, The Taming of the Shrew, Twelfth Night,* and *Richard III.* In one season, *The Merry Wives of Windsor* was the comedy of choice for four directors at festivals stretching from California to Maine, with Ohio and Vermont in between. But oddities also attract: the difficult tragicomedy, *Troilus and Cressida,* was chosen by three different directors one summer.

Major festivals like the two Stratfords tend to engage directors who already have established reputations. In Canada, such talents as the late Sir Tyrone Guthrie, Michael Langham, Jean Gascon, John Hirsch, Peter Coe, and Douglas Campbell have worked with equally distinguished casts. In Connecticut, Michael Kahn, Cyril Ritchard, Stephen Porter, Ellis Rabb, Joseph Anthony, Edwin Sherin, John Dexter, and Word Baker have exercised talents already well known on Broadway. San Diego, though not a large, wealthy festival, has had its quota of well known directors. Among them: Ellis Rabb, Stephen Porter, William Ball, Mel Shapiro, Allen Fletcher, and the late B. Iden Payne.

Although the New York Shakespeare Festival can attract famed directors, many of whom might be eager for the opportunity to work in Central Park, Lincoln Center, or the Festival's Astor Place theatre-complex, producer Joseph Papp has consistently been more interested in encouraging and developing new, young directorial talent. This is in line with his policy of supplementing Shakespeare with the works of new, young playwrights and staging all of them predominantly with the talents of new, young performers.

As honey attracts bears, so successful directors seem to attract noted stars. Given the basic desire—indeed, need—to play favorite Shakespearean roles, stars have a concomitant desire: to realize the parts only under the guidance of a really skillful, appreciative director. Some of the bears and bees drawn to Stratford's Canadian directorial honey have included Christopher Plummer, Kate Reid, Martha Henry, Alan Bates, Donald Davis, William Hutt, Douglas Rain, and Len Cariou. In Connecticut, the sweet bait attracted such names as Jessica Tandy, Raymond Massey, Alfred Drake, Jack Palance, Christopher Plummer, Mildren Dunnock, Morris Carnovsky, Nina Foch, Katharine Hepburn, June Havoc, Kim Hunter, Lillian Gish, Eva LeGallienne, Ruby Dee, and Robert Ryan. All in all, these are something like rolls of honor of Canadian and American players. The festivals can be glad that Shakespeare is such good bait, both for directors and performers.

Much Ado About Design

Settings, costumes, lighting, and makeup for Shakespeare

The Stratford Festival of Canada: *Love's Labour's Lost*. Designed by Sam Kirkpatrick. Lighting by Gil Wechsler.

Shakespeare himself probably was not too concerned about set and costume design for his plays, but Shakespeare festivals honoring his name in North America make "much ado about" scenery, costuming, lighting, and makeup. While Elizabethan staging practice used elaborate and fashionable gowns, cloaks, and crowns, the scenery was mostly limited to banners and hangings—plus appropriate prop pieces such as beds and thrones. Stylish garb or romanticized classical costuming, very simple suggestion of the play's locales, and numerous scene changes in front of the permanent architectural façade of the stage house constituted the general design look of the Elizabethan plays.

For the 20th Century ensemble staging Shakespeare, it is a major design task just to recreate the look of Elizabethan England—should the company wish to evoke the visual quality of Shakespeare's own theatre. But, more than that, it is seldom that any self-respecting contemporary Shakespeare festival can leave Shakespeare alone. Not content to let a work be played in its original period costume, festivals continually attempt to make the play more "relevant," and more interesting to a contemporary audience.

Thus, in one summer, *As You Like It*—originally set in the Elizabethan never-never land of the Forest of Arden—will appear at the New York Shakespeare Festival with characters outfitted for a meeting of aristocrats from Napoleonic France and Byronic England in the Bois de Boulogne. The same show, at the New Jersey Shakespeare Festival, can take on the appearance of a fairy tale version of medieval England—which seems not too far removed from Robin Hood and the Sheriff of Nottingham romping in Sherwood Forest. And, the Alabama Shakespeare Festival is not loath to create a cross between hillbilly Appalachia and the Son-of-*Godspell* for their own version of *As You Like It*.

Much Ado About Nothing seems equally at home in an early 20th Century-Teddy Roosevelt America production, as it does set in the mid-19th Century-*Gone with the Wind*-South. Most companies have tried their hand at staging in modern dress. Some costumes are elaborate "Paris" creations, others might have a chic, New York, 7th Avenue look. Still others use rehearsal clothes—black trousers and turtleneck sweaters—to help a group and an audience get back to basic Shakespeare: his words.

Once the director and the actor have done their work of interpreting what the audience will hear and how they will understand the words, the physical production falls into four areas: lighting, costuming, setting, and makeup. The designers in these fields create what the audience actually sees on the stage. Each festival has its own approach to design elements. Some festivals give a full treatment to both settings and costuming. Others use less scenery and rely heavily on elaborate costuming. Elaborate design in any or all of the visual fields has as much to do with the size of the festival budget, the degree of professionalism of the designers that can be afforded, and the number of technical crew, as it does with the kind of theatre and the circumstances in which the ensemble is performing.

Sometimes a company with a minimal production budget, eager crew, and resourceful designers will create a wonderful group of costumes. Other times highly funded groups who have the ability to purchase the best, may not be successful in their chosen design concept. Much of what happens from a design point of view is influenced by the kind of theatre in which a group performs. Community auditoriums can demand an entirely different production look than an outdoor amphitheatre.

But indoors or out, there are two elements of most productions that do not receive the attention they deserve: lighting and makeup. Concern about the quality of the lighting was not foremost in the Eli-

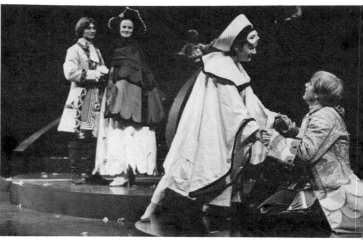

The Colorado Shakespeare Festival: *Hamlet (top)*; Sets: Dan Dryden; Costumes: Deborah Dryden; Lighting: Richard Riddell. The Oregon Shakespearean Festival: *The Two Gentlemen of Verona (above)*; Costumes: Jean Davidson.

zabethan stagings, either. At the outdoor theatres, performances took place in mid-afternoon, eliminating the necessity of lighting. If a production was played indoors—for example, at court—room candles, torches, and tapers provided the illumination. At the North American Shakespeare festivals, the quality and quantity of lighting seems to be in direct relation to the festival budget.

The New York Shakespeare Festival, the American Shakespeare Theatre, and the Stratford Festival of Canada all have resident lighting designers using professional approaches. In other locations, low budgets mean that a major outlay for lighting equipment cannot be afforded. Frequently, small groups suffer from insufficient equipment. Outdoor theatres like the Oregon Shakespearean Festival, the New York Shakespeare Festival, and the Utah Shakespeare Festival all have specially built stands and control booths; the San Francisco Shakespeare Festival (while it was still in Marin County) hung its equipment from conveniently placed tree branches. Utah's approach to lighting is, in their own words, "traditional by its nature"; and in their new theatre facilities they feel they have provided "what seems merely to be competent rather than anything special. We feel we have achieved the latter, however, in what we see as a very special aesthetic synthesis of carefully planned lighting positions within the Tudor architecture of the plant."

In most theatrical productions, lighting—which is the most necessary design element—is paradoxically the least noticeable. Shakespeare's plays were not written for elaborate lighting effects—the equipment and the techniques were unknown. Although, in retrospect, there are many moments for dramatic illumination and special lighting effects. But, as in theatre generally, concern about lighting runs second to the major visual elements of costuming and settings.

Perhaps the most criminal neglect in the North

The Utah Shakespearean Festival: *Macbeth* (top); Witches' mask and hands designed by Elizabeth Pilcher. The Theatre at Monmouth: *As You Like It* (left); Court dresses for Celia and Rosalind designed by Burton Bell.

American Shakespeare festivals' design is that of makeup. It is not a neglect unique to the Shakespeare festivals, but one that is fairly widespread throughout threatrical circles. It is seldom that a makeup designer is required in a Shakespeare festival. Special effects like the design of Ariel's or Caliban's faces are usually done by the costume designer so that the face painting will be consistent with the costume painting.

Unfortunately, in many North American Shakespeare festivals, the youth of student actors, combined with a lack of training in the fine points of makeup, which plagues American drama in general, creates a poor quality of stage face. Most actors are fairly adept at applying the proper amount of greasepaint, eyeliners, eye shadow or lip rouge to ensure that their own facial features will carry farther than the 5th row. Beyond that, however, they are at a loss. It is seldom that a young actor is sufficiently versed in his craft to create a subtle old age makeup.

Essentially, however, it seems that the American actor is either unwilling or improperly trained to stand back from the role he/she is playing. The actor does not ask what "should" this person look like, and then proceed to alter his/her own features to fit some ideal concept. Basically, the lack of care and concern with makeup is a minor matter. But, because it is a minor matter, it is continually ignored. Directors and designers concerned with the appearance of their productions should not only demand more, but also give more, in the way of direction.

The role that scenery plays in Shakespeare festival design stands in a special relationship to both the type of theatre structure and the budget. Festivals with Elizabethan theatre reconstructions have permanent scenery of a special kind. Hofstra University, Columbus College (Georgia), the Oregon Shakespearean Festival, the Utah, Odessa (Texas), and San Diego Festivals all limit their scenery to small prop pieces. The Elizabethan stage house provided the necessary variety of inner-above and inner-below staging areas. The Folger Theatre Group, which works on a permanent reconstructed evocation of an Elizabethan theatre, is just as likely to entirely mask the house with another setting, as it is to use the house in pure Elizabethan form. A Folger Theatre Group *Twelfth Night* filled the entire stage with a mylar geodesic dome, while its circus *Romeo and Juliet* parked gypsy wagons on stage.

Outdoor theatres without the permanent Elizabethan setting find themselves dealing with other problems. When Ming Cho Lee was resident designer at the New York Shakespeare Festival, he turned waterproof, and windproof, metal pipes, ramps, and ladders into multi-leveled unit settings. Somehow the settings, which were frequently compared to erector-set construction, managed to maintain a basic quality of the Shakespearean stage. Santo Loquasto, who has been the designer since the 1973 summer season in New York, has created a heavily textured *As You Like It* setting that also maintained the basic double-leveled playing area so consistent with Elizabethan playhouses. For another Delacorte Theatre production, *King Lear,* Loquasto created a monumental setting by completing the fortress-like quality of the theatre with a back wall and a level, light wood, rectangular thrust stage. When the back wall portals swung open, the nearby Central Park pond also seemed part of the setting.

At the Sylvan Theatre in Washington, D.C., home of the Summer Shakespeare Festival, designers are faced with a tremendous problem of scale. Anything that is designed for their outdoor stage must blend in with, but not be overpowered by, the Washington Monument and other federal edifices.

At the University of Colorado's Mary Rippon Theatre, Colorado Shakespeare Festival designers used to be faced with yet another problem of scale.

The Oregon Shakespearean Festival: *Love's Labour's Lost*

The astroturf-covered stage, surrounded by three-story, pseudo-Renaissance buildings, was the size of a small football field. Their Festival budget did not permit the kind of stage construction which would fill the entire space. Nor did they seem satisfied with the several attempts at limiting the size of the stage—either by using small unit settings or enclosing a space with 18-foot screens. For some inexplicable reason, both the Festival producers and many local critics seemed most happy with that space when it was left open, and the scenery was confined to the bench-and-banner-school of stage design. The Colorado Shakespeare Festival could not help but benefit from a serious reassessment of their stage size, theatre sightlines, and the best way to design for them. In the 1974 season a unit setting was tried once again at the Colorado festival.

Festivals that make their home in community auditoriums or newly designed theatres can rely on neither a setting of natural beauty nor a permanent half-timbered façade. They find themselves building new settings for each season, sometimes for each production. Most of these indoor festivals have a resident scene designer for the entire season. Often the summer Shakespeare set designer spends his winters teaching theatre at universities and colleges, although the most professional festivals, such as the two Stratfords and New York, hire designers who usually work in regional and New York theatre.

Resident scene designers at the Kansas Shakespeare Festival and the Alabama Shakespeare Festival have provided multi-use unit settings. Modularized, the elements can be rearranged, and create a new look for each of the season's productions. In practice, however, this economical theory has yet to be applied with great flair and ingenuity. Touring Shakespeare companies must, of course always design with an eye to travel flexibility. Professional Shakespeare festivals such as the Great Lakes Festival, the Stratford Festival of Canada, or the American Shakespeare Theatre, frequently hire a different designer for each production. The quality of the work is professional; the houses resemble familiar commercial Broadway and regional theatres. The work is creative, well constructed, well executed, and gives the designer a chance to try his hand at creating a setting which will provide the adaptability, the flexibility, the openness, the lack of definition, with all the potential that the staging of Shakespeare demands.

Costuming takes the starring role in the design work at Shakespeare festivals. Whether playing before an Elizabethan reconstruction, in a modern theatre, or before nature's own backdrop, the cast has to be clothed. In fact, because of the many difficulties and varieties of the stage setting, most festivals rely on the costuming to create the place, time, and atmosphere. The costuming carries the mood and is the most visible manifestation of the director's interpretation.

At the festivals with borderline funding, the majority of the production budget goes into costuming. Costumes are relied upon to solve any questions that sketchy settings might leave in the audience's mind. Most festivals have found it is necessary, both for considerations of time and for consistency of design, to hire a resident designer for an entire season. In many places, the same costumer comes back season after season. Familiarity with the local resources for buying materials, firsthand knowledge of the facilities of the theatre's costume shop (if they are built in-house), plus a close acquaintanceship with the costume stock remaining from previous productions, enable the costume designer to use every cent of the costume budget in an economical fashion.

Under the auspices of resident designer Jane Greenwood, one of the most ingenious dollar stretching plans has been set up for the American

Shakespeare Theatre. Each season, Jane Greenwood designs the costumes; then the theatre turns its costume budget over to Brooks Van Horn, a New York costume house which builds the garments. Sometimes the theatre's budget covers costs; other seasons it does not. Brooks Van Horn builds to the American Shakespeare Theatre's specifications, and the theatre uses the costumes for the student and summer season. Then the costumes go into the Brooks Van Horn stock which is available for rental by theatres across the country. In that way, the Connecticut theatre gets the costumes they want, and Brooks van Horn makes up any funds lost in the construction from the rental profits.

The resident designers' responsibilities are various: they design their own shows, and in theatres such as the Utah Festival, they also oversee the work of guest designers. At the Alabama Shakespeare Festival, the resident designer also co-ordinates the costumes that are rented from costume houses in New York or Atlanta. For costumes built at the festival location, materials are purchased in town at the Alabama Festival; in nearby Denver for the Colorado Festival. For the Utah Festival's costumes, pre-season buying is carried out in San Francisco, Los Angeles, or Salt Lake City by designer Barbara Cox. When designer Peg Kellner needs something special for the San Diego National Festival, she usually shops in Los Angeles. The Theatre at Monmouth designer, Burton Bell, searches New England factory outlet stores for his materials.

Where the costumes are actually built depends on the physical facilities of the festival theatre. Those associated with a university usually borrow the university theatre costume shop. The New York Shakespeare Festival's shop is in the downtown, Public Theatre building. The Alabama Shakespeare Festival constructed their costumes on one sewing machine that was set up nearby the theatre.

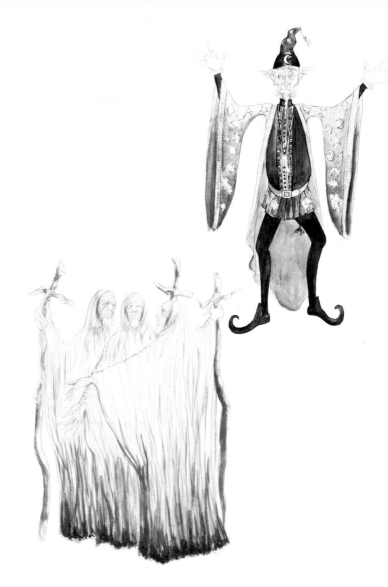

The Utah Shakespearean Festival: Costume designs by Elizabeth Pilcher for Pinch in *The Comedy of Errors* (top) and Witches in *Macbeth* (above).

Most festival costume designers come from the academic community. They might teach costume history or costume construction during the winter months. Some festival designers work for Off-Off-Broadway groups the rest of the year. Others work with resident theatre companies that are dark during the summer months. Some work in professional theatre most of the year. Theoni Aldredge, who has been the busiest of resident designers at the New York Shakespeare Festival, also finds time to do film work. The American Shakespeare Theatre designer Jane Greenwood works on Broadway, in regional theatre, or in Europe for the months she is not occupied with the Stratford theatre.

Designing season after season of Shakespeare, the resident designer becomes somewhat an expert in recreating the Elizabethan silhouette. Some festivals are known for being sticklers about exact period details—right down to the proper hip rolls, undergarments, and seaming detail. Other theatres are concerned with capturing the basic outline and do not concern themselves with minute designer details. At the Colorado Shakespeare Festival, the concern was less with faithful period detail and more with making the costume material, decoration, and detailing of sufficiently large scale to be in proportion to their large stage. While at the Utah Shakespearean Festival there are only two guidelines for costumers. One—to keep in mind the nature of the building, "its natural wood and stucco, against which their costumes will play." Second—the designer is limited in historical periods "to those that would have been known to Shakespeare's day. The designer still has a great deal of freedom in terms of period—the span is from Egyptian to Jacobean."

However, thanks to the North American Shakespeare festival habit of reinterpreting the time and place of Shakespeare's plays, it is seldom that a resident designer finds him/herself repeating designs in frequent Elizabethan productions. Over a period of several seasons, a designer might find him/herself designing *Macbeth* for 11th Century Scotland or 16th Century England. *The Merchant of Venice* is just as likely to be in a Jet Set 1973 Venice, as it is in Renaissance Italy. *Coriolanus* could be done in true Roman style or World War II Italian. *Julius Caesar* is as valid in modern dress as in Roman toga.

The quality of Shakespeare festival stage design—as is true for all theatre—is directly tied to subtle relationships between director and designers. An excellent director with strong visual sense can push and pull until a mediocre designer evolves a very special set solution. A strong designer can sweep a less visually oriented director along. When the non-visual director works with the mediocre designer on a minimal budget the audience will usually get cheated out of a truly thorough and professionally presented design concept.

Currently in the festival complex, one of the most felicitous relationships seems to be that between the American Shakespeare Theatre's artistic director, Michael Kahn, and his resident costumer, Jane Greenwood. They have been working together since 1966. Greenwood points out that Kahn is one of those "visual" directors. He will want a production of *Merry Wives of Windsor* to look like a black and white Elizabethan woodcut; or perhaps a *Measure for Measure* should capture the quality of Hogarth's paintings. From that point it is the designer's job to manifest the visual concept.

Nonetheless, big budget or small, recent graduate designer or professional with many years of experience, it makes little difference. When the lights dim, the stunningly designed, carefully constructed sets and costumes pale beside the carefully turned phrases, plots, and plays of William Shakespeare.

Shakespeare in Easy Stages

Designing and adapting theatres for producing Elizabethan plays

The only known sketch of an outdoor Elizabethan stage: The Swan Theatre (1596) by Arend van Buchell, based on eye-witness report of Johannes de Witt

A variety of theatre structures and stage-shapes are used in the United States and Canada for the production of Shakespeare's plays. Of these, quasi-Elizabethan theatres are fairly numerous. Since more fantasy than accuracy is involved in the design of such playhouses, the claims of some of them to be "replicas," or even "the world's most authentic replica," should be viewed with either indulgence or suspicion, depending on the festival visitor's feelings about Shakespeare scholarship.

Fortunately for those Shakespeare festivals which use modern evocations of the Globe or the Fortune, the basic elements of its multiple stage areas work very well in production. They make possible swift transitions from scene to scene and eliminate the need for acres of scenery and tons of props. So well, in fact, do the varied areas and levels serve the Bard's texts, that more than one director or designer has been moved to comment that, if the Globe wasn't like John Cranford Adams' or C. Walter Hodges' visions of it, then it certainly *ought* to have been so.

What a sensational coup it would be for some Shakespearean scholar to find an authentic drawing of the Globe Theatre hidden away in an old trunk in a Stratford-upon-Avon attic! Or, possibly a detailed description of the Globe and how it was used in staging Shakespeare's dramas, in the Bard's own handwriting.

Dreams, idle dreams! It is true that some rare and valuable old drawings and writings have been discovered in this century, shedding light on art and life in past eras. That could happen again. But, as theatre historians Oscar Brockett and Brooks McNamara have noted, not very much conclusive information about Shakespeare's Globe Theatre has surfaced since the disappearance of the first and the second Globe structures in 1613 and 1644, respectively.

It is significant that when David Garrick engineered the first great festival salute to Shakespeare in 1769 in Stratford-upon-Avon, he did not attempt to recreate a Globe Theatre. Instead, he caused a Rotunda to be constructed as the major scene of the events of his disastrous Shakespeare Jubilee. Neither the first Stratford Festival Memorial Theatre, opened in 1879, nor the present playhouse, dedicated in 1932, were designed to evoke an authentic Shakespearean theatre.

Curiously, the passion for building replicas of the Globe Theatre seems to be a distinctly American phenomenon. In 1912, London had its first "Globe Theatre" since the 17th Century, and it was thanks to the energy and imagination of a Brooklyn-born lady. The lady was none other than Lady Randolph Churchill, mother of Sir Winston Churchill and raised in New York as Jennie Jerome. This Globe and a "Fortune Playhouse" which complemented it were temporary structures for a cultural event staged in the Earl's Court Exhibition Hall. For this project, called "Shakespeare's England," Lady Randolph had the distinguished architect Sir Edward Luytens design the theatres. Then, as now, no one knew with any certainty what the Globe may have looked like, so Luytens' work must have been an act of faith. Today, over half a century later, another American, the actor-director Sam Wanamaker, is moving ahead with plans for a *Third* Globe, to be built near the original London Bankside site. It will imitate neither Shakespeare's first nor second Globe.

The absence of authoritative details about the stage and playhouse used for many of Shakespeare's dramas has by no means discouraged the construction of modern theatres which purport or pretend to be replicas, reconstructions, or evocations of the First Globe. In some cases, the interest in rebuilding or reconstituting the Globe has been largely scholarly or antiquarian—to see, in models or life-sized in three dimensions, how Shakespeare's theatre or a typical Elizabethan playhouse may have looked. In some notable instances, however, the impetus has been merely to create acting and audience areas which could evoke the intimate ambience of the Elizabethan stage.

Only one rough sketch of an open-air Elizabethan stage survives. And, in fact, it survives only in a copy, since the original (1596) by Johannes de Witt was lost. This drawing represents the Swan Theatre (c. 1595), and it is still the subject of lively dispute and interpretation regarding what it may depict. Construction contracts for the Hope (1613) and the Fortune (1600) have been preserved. Also useful for scholarly speculation have been three small and rather ambiguous 17th Century book illustrations, showing portions of stages. Brooks McNamara points out, however, that many references in Elizabethan play texts, in diaries, and in official records have enlarged the store of knowledge.

Nonetheless, much of what has been written about the Globe and her sister playhouses remains largely fascinating, thoughtful conjecture. John Cranford Adams' *The Globe Playhouse* (1942) offered a detailed reconstruction which seems to be the basis of most of the extant "Globe Theatres," though the Thomas Wood Stevens–B. Iden Payne version built temporarily in Chicago (1933) and copied in San Diego (1935) preceded Adams' theorizing. C. Walter Hodges, in *The Globe Restored* (1953), presented his educated guesses, which were attractive and playable. The Adams conception was forcefully attacked in Alois Nagler's *Shakespeare's Stage* (1958) and in Leslie Hotson's *Shakespeare's Wooden O* (1959).

An entry in the *Reader's Encyclopedia of Shakespeare* states the status of knowledge this way: ". . . all that we know of the playhouse for certain is that it had a thatched roof over the upper gallery and that certain of its dimensions were the same as those of the Fortune Theatre."

Five American Shakespeare stages still proclaim their kinship with the original Globe. These are: 1) the Hofstra University Globe, 2) the Globe in Columbus, Georgia, 3) the Globe of the Great Southwest, in Odessa, Texas, 4) the Old Globe Theatre, in San Diego, California, and, 5) the Globe Theatre in Los Angeles.

The Hofstra Globe is not a permanent theatre. It is a copy of the Globe theorized by John Cranford Adams, President Emeritus of Hofstra University. Actually only the stage portion has been constructed. Originally, it was designed for use each spring in the former Hofstra gymnasium. With the erection of the Hofstra Playhouse, it was then adapted to insertion in the conventional proscenium frame, with a modified thrust-stage over the orchestra pit. Photographs of Dr. Adams' Globe model, now in the Folger Shakespeare Library in Washington, D.C., show quite clearly the basis for the Hofstra stage. This concept has had much influence, not only on the creation of other "Globe Theatres," but also on some modern thrust stages and special scene designs for Shakespeare productions.

In the Adams model, the "outer stage" or main acting area juts out into the pit where the "groundlings" stood. This stage permits spectators to surround it on three sides. It contains some trapdoors for apparitions, descents into Hell, and burials. Two pillars support a roof which partially protects the performers from rain. Under this roof is an attic—the "Heavens"—from which props could be lowered to the stage and in which certain sound-effects

New York Shakespeare Festival's outdoor Delacorte **Theatre stage design by Santo Loquasto** for *King Lear* incorporates Central Park's lake and New York's skyline as part of the vista.

might be made. At the upper stage right and stage left corners of the thrust stage, there are entrance-exit doors, set at an angle to the stage. The doors can be closed or left open, depending on scenic needs. Upstage, there is an "inner stage," closed off by a curtain. Above this is a balcony, and immediately behind that, another curtained stage. These two pocket-stages are often called the "inner below" and the "inner above." (Some scholars insist that they are figments of Dr. Adams' imagination and, if used with the supposed semi-circular gallery seating at the Globe, would have made it difficult if not impossible for many spectators to see some important scenes. In a conventional modern orchestra-balcony seating plan such as that at Hofstra, however, there is no problem about sight-lines, and these "inner" areas provide effective variation and emphasis in staging, as well as making a swifter pace of performance possible.) Above the stage doors and adjacent to the balcony are two windows, stage right and stage left, which can also be played. Above the balcony area is another, smaller gallery, supposedly used by the theatre's musicians.

Possible uses of Dr. Adams' Globe and those proposed by Hodges and other theorists have been persuasively examined by such scholars as Bernard Beckerman, in *Shakespeare at the Globe,* and Ronald Watkins, in *On Producing Shakespeare.* Juliet's Balcony and Cleopatra's Monument, for example, can be easily staged, using the upper level of the Hofstra Globe. Shakespeare productions at Hofstra are not always set in the Adams Globe. When they are, however, impressive costumes, banners, properties, and small set-pieces are the major visual clues to a sense of place, time, and atmosphere.

The Odessa Globe of the Great Southwest attempts to suggest an Elizabethan exterior as well as to recreate the Bard's stage. The basic Adams elements have been inserted into a proscenium frame, as at Hofstra. They can be removed and stored, but producer-director Charles McCally prefers to leave them in place, owing to crew costs and the time involved. Also, the Globe idea of various neutral acting areas permits the multiple spaces to be used to good advantage with modern plays as well as with Shakespeare's masterworks. The Odessa claim to historical authenticity rests on the possibly unwise response of Allardyce Nicoll to founder Marjorie Morris' proposal to recreate the Globe in West Texas. Dr. Nicoll's comment: "You have reached for the stars, and you have found them. If you complete this theatre—and I believe you will—you will have the most nearly authentic replica of Shakespeare's own Globe anywhere on earth." At least that is the way Dr. Nicoll is quoted in Odessa.

In Columbus, Georgia, the Globe replica is composed of a center section "study" and "upper chamber" as well as bay windows right and left, with two large doors below the windows. This center section measures about 35 feet across, 29 feet high and 10 feet deep and, rolls into place on the college stage. The two wing sections also roll into place. A cupola section is added to the top of the center section. Facing roof pieces, plus doors, drapery, tapestries, and paintings complete this Globe Theatre. Using John C. Adam's book *The Globe Playhouse,* William P. Crowell was responsible for the design.

San Diego's Old Globe was the child of Thomas Wood Stevens' brain, and precedes the publication of Adams' book by almost a decade. A number of the ideas found in both visions of the Globe were already current among Shakespeare experts, however. The San Diego structure was originally more like its prototype than most of the alleged copies, in at least one respect. It was open to the sunny summer skies of Southern California. But even the Old Globe had to be roofed over, when it came into use for year-round production. Eventually, it also lost its distinc-

The Oregon Shakespearean Festival: *Troilus and Cressida*
on the indoor Angus Bowmer Theatre modern end stage

The Shakespeare Festival of Dallas sets up their summer stage in front of the park's bandshell.

tive Elizabethan stage carpentry, which was replaced with a more generalized suggestion of the multiple areas. This was partly dictated by the need to use the stage for modern plays.

Considering the various problems facing the would-be "reconstructor" of Shakespeare's Globe, the experience—and practice—of one of them may be instructive. He is R. Thad Taylor, founder and executive producer of The Shakespeare Society of America at the Globe Theatre, a Los Angeles based organization.

"I had long talks with C. Walter Hodges and Tyrone Guthrie, as well as with Sam Wanamaker and dozens of other scholars and directors," he says. "I weighed each opinion carefully, but depended mostly on my own judgment as an engineer to re-construct my Globe model."

Interestingly, Guthrie strongly advised Taylor *against* reproducing a replica, suggesting instead a modern theatre—which was just what Guthrie did for Canada's Stratford. Louis Marder, editor of the *Shakespeare Newsletter,* warned Taylor about the various scholarly disputes regarding the Globe. Taylor profited from study of such basic visual sources as the *Roxana* vignette of 1632, the *Messalina* vignette of 1640, and Vischer's View of London (1616). The Fortune contract was also helpful, as were the researches of Albright, Thorndike, and Cranford Adams. Of the latter's work, Taylor says, "I believe that his model is one of the best concepts ever done."

It boils down," Taylor agrees, "to my half-scale model being a 'composite Globe,' borrowing a little from all the known facts—and a few instances where imaginary forces must work. If one is to undertake the task of building a Globe Theatre, however, it must be a one-man-in-charge thing—and that's it—or one will never get the job done."

There is a second group of Elizabethan theatre "reconstructions" which are much more circumspect in their historical claims. Although the Adams Memorial Theatre in Cedar City, Utah, is often referred to by citizens and Festival visitors as a replica of the Globe Theatre, the Festival's producing director Fred Adams and his colleague, Douglas Cook, are careful to avoid such statements. Adams says it is "an *interpretation* of the John Cranford Adams Globe." That is an interesting way to explain what seems to be a mixture of th theories of Cranford Adams and C. Walter Hodges, with a lot of creative imagination as a catalyst.

The stage-house portion of the Adams Memorial was inaugurated in the 1972 season. The permanent pit, loge, and balcony seating were completed for the 1974 season. Some scholars think the Globe had an octagonal exterior. The Cedar City playhouse is hexagonal, to ensure unimpaired sight-lines. The seating is modern, simple, and relatively comfortable. No effort has been made to recreate Elizabethan benches or pit standing-room. Thanks to the warm, dry summers of Southern Utah, it is possible to leave the pit-area open to the sky, as was the Elizabethan practice. That is not to suggest that London, in the days of good Queen Bess, had a climate like that of the American Southwest. Far from it. During the outdoor season, plays—like modern baseball games—occasionally had to be called on account of rain. Nor were the Globe and her open-air sister theatres used in the depths of winter.

The stage house of the Adams Memorial is unusual in that it has a generous expanse of roof extending over the thrust stage. This effectively eliminates the pillars and painted Heavens of the Cranford Adams model. Instead of an elaborate ceiling, painted with Zodiacal signs and containing traps for raising and lowering props, the overhang is completely open, revealing heavy wooden trusses and a number of lighting instruments. Whatever this arrangement may

Shakespeare at Winedale performs in a 19th Century Texas barn

forfeit in period atmosphere, it makes up in efficiency in lighting the multiple stage areas. The walls of the stage house suggest the timber-and-plaster construction methods popular in Tudor times and before. In Cedar City, the plaster portions are actually heavy laminated wood panels, coated with a glaze of mellow yellow paint and pebbling. This can be a bad light-reflector, so illumination either has to be toned down when it falls on the panels, or panel-plugs with more subdued colors or special scenic designs have to be fitted over the basic wall covering.

At the Folger Shakespeare Library in the nation's capital, there is also an Elizabethan theatre. It is handsome, solidly built, like a variation of the Cranford Adams vision which it predates. It is inside the imposing library-museum complex. Fitted into a lofty space with a rectangular ground-plan, it does not try to imitate octagons, hexagons, or wooden O's. Designed by Paul Cret for Henry Clay Folger, the library's founder and principal benefactor, the theatre was for a long time used only as a three-dimensional exhibit of an educated guess about the structure of an Elizabethan playhouse.

The dressing-rooms and other practical theatre accommodations make it quite clear that Folger wanted his architect to build a theatre that could be used. Originally, however, zoning ordinances and fire laws forbade that. Today, thanks to the production program of the Folger Theatre Group, these original intentions are being honored. And, while the ensemble has shown no inclination to do cycles of the Shakespeare canon for school classes, at least one Shakepearean play is staged each season. For several of these, the Folger set-designers have taken pains to suppress, hide, or ignore the distinctive architectural elements of this charming Elizabethan evocation.

In Oregon's Ashland, Shakespeare is saluted on the open-air Elizabethan stage with productions which strive for a kind of period authenticity, without sacrificing visual imagination and variety. The current playhouse is the third of its kind on the site. The Festival designer, Richard Hay, who outlined the basic stage elements and the Tudor decor for the architects, says it is based on the specifications of the contract for the Fortune Theatre. Some of the Cranford Adams ideas were incorporated, and the decoration was adapted from Elizabethan period examples.

No attempt has been made to carry period authenticity beyond the stage. The audience sits in firm wooden seats in a raked amphitheatre, with no galleries. Sturdy pipe-frames at either side of the front rows of seats support a large number of lighting instruments. Lights on the stage itself are cleverly concealed.

Designer Hay discusses the way in which Ashland's period stage is used to approximate Elizabethan production practices: "In recent years, we have been working with a fixed facade for all the plays. This façade really has eliminated inner stages as adjunct proscenium stages to the main thrust stage. So we really don't use the inner stages, as such, any longer. They function primarily as an entrance onto the main acting area or onto the balcony area above. We have replaced the usual 'inner below' with a projecting pavilion. This also provides an upper level which projects in front of the 'inner above.' Below, it creates three entrances to the main stage. The central one can be concealed by a curtain. I have a particular objection to the use of the inner stages as small proscenium stages anyway. The audience, given the size of our house, cannot see or hear very well what may be going on in them."

Whether or not Cranford Adams and Hodges are essentially correct in their basic assumptions about the nature of Shakespeare's stage, the various "Globes" and the modern multiple area stages which have been derived from the theorizing make possible a number of effective solutions to the problems posed in staging the comedies, chronicles, and tragedies of the Elizabethan period.

Thanks to the variety of levels and playing spaces provided by the modern stage evocations, scenes involving relatively large groups of people can follow each other—or alternate with intimate dramatic passages requiring no more than two or three players—in rapid succession. While a royal court is still grandly moving off the main stage through the stage right door, a rabble of beggars may be tumbling through the stage left door in full cry. Or a tender love scene may be in progress on the balcony level above. Using the areas, virtually no scenery, and a minimum of properties, it is possible for effectively costumed performers to set and dress the stage with their persons, to bring the plot and characters to vibrant life, and to maintain a fairly brisk pace and a coherent playing rhythm. These are especially important if a Shakespearean drama is to have maximum impact. If the flow of the action is interrupted by scene changes or by the time consumed while one set of characters exits as another group waits to enter, the rhythm can be destroyed, and audience interest is apt to be diverted. Modern audiences, notably American ones, tend to be impatient with long theatre evenings. Thus, at those festivals where uncut Shakespeare is a goal, the more briskly and uninterruptedly the play flows along, the more it will carry its audience along with it. At Ashland, for example, the purist policy calls for virtually complete texts to be played. Generally, the tempo and coherence is such—strongly assisted by the multiple areas

The Hofstra Shakespeare Festival alternates the use of their Cranford Adams' Globe reconstruction with the University's proscenium stage: *Richard III (right top).* The Colorado Shakespeare Festival Joseph Zender design for a unit set that fits into their Mary Rippon Theatre *(right).*

of the Elizabethan stage—that this can be accomplished in three-hour spans, without intermissions and without any noticeable grumbling or loss of attention from the audience.

In yet another example of America's Shakespeare Complex, the Globe Theatre has even been invoked to help celebrate the Bicentennial and the American past. At Busch Gardens, only a few miles from Colonial Williamsburg, an "enlarged" Globe has been constructed to help recreate the "yesteryear romance and essence" of various typical European villages in England, France, and Germany from which many American immigrants came.

The Gardens' theme is "The Old Country," and the Globe is seen as its focal point. As such an important component in the $30 million family entertainment park, the Globe has been designed as a multi-purpose reconstruction. August Busch III, president of Anheuser-Busch, notes: "It is designed for year-round use; not only for drama, but for conventions and private gatherings."

Opening in the spring of 1975, the Globe has a novel major attraction in the high tourist season: "A multisensory show of illusions and magic, centered around popular Shakespearean characters." This suggests that the plays themselves are regarded as beyond the grasp of the summer tourist. Perhaps, in imitation of Disney World, but instead of Mickey Mouse, the Busch Globe could have Hamlet and Ophelia as live hosts!

Because Williamsburg has long been a year-round tourist and convention center, the Globe will be the scene of more traditional Shakespeare stagings when summer is past. A Shakespeare Festival, Busch concedes, is a definite possibility, but no decision has yet been made.

The new, improved Busch Globe is supposedly the result of detailed research. Larry Millis, of Peckham-Guyton, St. Louis architects for the project, agrees that there are a number of question marks about the Globe. Most of the architectural research was done at the University of Illinois Library, where theatre and architectural histories were consulted and conjectural Globe models studied.

Millis says, "The Globe is believed to have been polygonal in shape. Our version will take the shape of an elongated octagon. It will be larger than the first Globe—to accommodate more visitors. We have also added a lobby that did not originally exist." Shakespeare would be astonished.

Lessons learned from experiments with quasi-Elizabethan stage effects in London at the Old Vic and in Edinburgh at the Assembly Hall convinced the late Sir Tyrone Guthrie of the value of the multiple area concept. For that reason, even when the Stratford Festival of Canada offered its first season in a tent in 1953, the stage was inspired by such Globe Theatre theorizing. Later, when the permanent Festival Theatre opened in 1957, the thrust stage remained the focal point of the auditorium. As originally conceived and developed by Guthrie and his designer Tanya Moiseiwitsch, the stage was to serve his belief that: "A play can be best presented by getting as near as possible to the manner in which the author envisaged its performance."

In 1961, Ms. Moiseiwitsch and Brian Jackson revised and simplified the stage. Today it is essentially a broad, deep thrust, surrounded through an arc of 220° around its five exposed sides with steeply sloped amphitheatre seating for some 2,260 people. Whether in the orchestra arc or in the balcony, no viewer is more than 65' from the thrust stage. The main playing area is flanked on the audience sides by four levels of broad steps which can be played or used for entrances from or exits into the vomitoria tunneled below the audience seating. Stage right and left, there are spacious doorways, approached by steps leading up to platform areas in front of them.

From these, further platforms and two sets of open stairs lead to the central upper level of a portico or balcony, supported by five pillars below. Central doorways, above and below, give access to the playing areas and also faintly suggest the Cranford Adams inner below and inner above. In all, there are seven acting levels and nine major entrances for this stage, as well as trap doors and other special effects. It is a permanent setting; indeed, aside from the players' costumes, a few banners, and some occasional pieces of furniture, it is all the setting that is needed, Shakespeare's appeal—at least in his own theatre—being more to the ears and the imagination than to the eyes. In neutral tones relieved by wood-graining, the Moiseiwitsch stage is the essence of architectural simplicity. Its success as a solution for Shakespeare staging problems, without getting producers into scholarly problems about authenticity, has subsequently inspired a number of theatres, among them that of the Chichester Festival in Sussex, England.

In the fall of 1973, when the New York Shakespeare Festival under Joseph Papp's leadership took over the Vivian Beaumont and the Forum Theatres in Lincoln Center, the latter became the Mitzi E. Newhouse Theatre and was adapted as a winter home for Shakespeare production. The Forum, owing to budget problems at the time the complex was first opened, had never really been finished, but it already had the basic outlines of the Stratford, Ontario, auditorium, with a thrust stage, limited entrances, and the possibility of constructing any kind of pavilion or scenic structure needed to dress the thrust. Papp and his design colleagues were quick to exploit the multiple area concept to the full in handsome, imaginative, unusual ways.

Under the Beaumont-Forum's previous director, Jules Irving, major Shakespeare productions were staged upstairs in the Beaumont. Much larger than the Forum stage, but with the same thrust-audience surround effect—plus a deep proscenium stage behind the thrust—the Beaumont offered many more possibilities for stage movement and design solutions in presenting the Shakespeare canon. These were intelligently exploited. Oddly enough, in spring 1975, Papp announced his intention to gut the Beaumont and rebuild it as a proscenium house.

The arena stage which served the Champlain Shakespeare Festival at the University of Vermont in Burlington before the 1974 opening of its Royall Tyler Theatre was capable of being modified into a long, rectangular thrust, when the seating at the end facing the entrance doors was replaced with a temporary stage structure. The new Tyler Theatre is much more flexible.

At Ashland, in addition to the open-air Elizabethan Theatre, Festival guests also have the opportunity to see the Bard's works staged indoors in the starkly modern Angus Bowmer Theatre. This theatre seems a transition between a thrust, with its semi-circular stepped seating, and a proscenium arch stage and its rows of orchestra seats out front. All of the seats are steeply inclined in the Bowmer so there are no problems with the sightlines. The rows curve gently around the fringes of what designer Richard Hay calls an "extended forestage in an open-end theatre." A basic multiple area setting—in any required period—*can* be constructed in the stage space, but it is just as easy to solve scenic problems with a temporarily installed turntable, or to provide an atmospherically and architecturally neutral empty space for the action of the drama. The back of the Bowmer's stage area opens up for shifting of scene wagons on and off. A stage elevator makes possible additional rapid shifting of stored set units from below stage level.

Cedar City's Adams Memorial and Ashland's Elizabethan Theatre are period open-air theatres, but there are other outdoor Shakespeare festival theatres which make no attempt to evoke the Globe or the Fortune. Among these are the New York Shakespeare Festival's summer home, the Delacorte Theatre in Central Park; the Sylvan Theatre, not far from the Washington Monument in the District of Columbia; and the Colorado Shakespeare Festival's handsome red-rock-benched Mary Rippon Theatre, enclosed on four sides by campus buildings in Italian Renaissance style.

Such theatres do not bind their designers and directors to any Elizabethan models or preconceptions. Indeed, it is often an easy solution—not to mention an inexpensive one—to erect a few neutral flats with some doorways on a raised stage and consider the stage as set. Or a rather conventional box-setting can be devised. The most daring and varied settings, as might be expected, have been those created for the New York Shakespeare Festival's Delacorte. More often than not, thanks to the semi-circular seating and the thrust stage, the multiple area concept is employed in some guise or other. Tyrone Guthrie's lessons were not learned in vain.

Those theatres which have proscenium arches—the large picture-frames behind which scenery may be "flown" up out of sight into the flies—can be deadly traps for Shakespearean production. The frame, with its customary curtain, can interpose a visible barrier between the players and the audience, destroying a valuable sense of intimacy and immediacy. The varied potentials for scene changes via flying, wagons, and other traditional means of set shifting encourage some designers to create a succession of pictorializations which can slow down the pace of the performance. Scenic designs which are too detailed or too complicated can also interfere with the impact and coherence of a production, distracting audiences.

Festivals which of necessity must perform in proscenium arch frames usually try to break out of the frame. If the stage already has an apron or forestage, action may be pushed to the very edge of this. If there is no apron, a temporary forestage may be built to create a modified thrust effect, even if some seats front and center have to be sacrificed, as is done for the Alabama Shakespeare Festival.

Designers often specify a multiple area stage set. This can be Elizabethan in appearance, or it may only abstract the levels and functions of such a stage solution. This has been used with notable success at the Great Lakes Shakespeare Festival. Originally, the multiple areas there were effectively those of an Elizabethan stage, but now settings are much more flexible, incorporating some of the basic elements only as needed.

The stage of the American Shakespeare Festival, in Stratford, Connecticut, is an uneasy compromise between a modified thrust and a proscenium stage. In this regard, it is much like the Royal Shakespeare Theatre in Stratford-upon-Avon. Again, the recreation of multiple acting areas and levels has often been the most effective solution to the problem of setting a multi-scened, large cast Shakespearean play, especially one of the histories.

Ashland's Richard Hay, after five years of designing for the cavernous proscenium theatre in Memorial Hall at Stanford University, in California, learned what Shakespeare and his fellows may have discovered by accident. These things he incorporated into his specifications for the Oregon Festival's Elizabethan and Bowmer Theatres: "Among the things, enclosing audience and actors in the same room. That is an important aesthetic quality; it is really essential to good theatre. For me, theatre is spatial, rather than pictorial."

It is interesting that most of the North American Shakespeare Festivals, in the way in which their stages are designed or adapted, seem to share this belief. Certainly the plays of Shakespeare and his contemporaries are well served by it.

Subsidizing Shakespeare

Underwriting festivals is more than a matter of money

The ticket-buying audience

Where are they now, those Shakespeare festivals which began so bravely and planned so hopefully? What has become, for instance, of the Bardic festival at Antioch College (Ohio) which succeeded in staging all of Shakespeare's plays before it faded away? Where is the Southern Shakespeare Repertory Theatre—sometimes called "Shakespeare in the Tropics"—of the University of Miami (Florida)? And the Cincinnati (Ohio) Shakespeare Festival at the Edgecliff Academy of Fine Arts: whatever became of it? Why did the Victoria (Texas) Shakespeare Festival disappear? What happened to the Southeastern Shakespeare Festival in Atlanta (Georgia), the Irish Hills (Michigan) Shakespeare Repertory Festival, and the Hollywood (California) Shakespeare Festival? For that matter, why did the California Shakespeare Festival disappear?

The answers are complex and varied. The Shakespeare venture at Antioch, under the direction of Arthur Lithgow, was invited to Cleveland, where it became the Great Lakes Shakespeare Festival. Subsequently, it was replaced with a different management. The Victoria undertaking lapsed when its producing director, Charles McCally, was called to the Globe of the Great Southwest, in Odessa, Texas. Other festivals have withered away from lack of audience support or insufficient subsidy. Or both.

Wanting to produce Shakespeare in a festival setting is not enough of an impetus to guarantee that such a venture, once begun, is going to prosper. It does seem to be true that Shakespeare, more than any other playwright in English—or any language, for that matter—is a remarkable box-office attraction. Even small communities such as Cedar City, in Southern Utah, have shown that a repertory of the Bard's plays will draw crowds year after year. But that doesn't mean that any small community, college or university, or any producing-director is automatically going to have success with a program of Shakespeare.

There are too many variables at work. Obviously the community and/or the local college has to be strongly supportive—rather than indifferent or actively hostile—of the festival. Clearly the director must have, in addition to artistic gifts and practical theatre experience, sufficient energy and charisma to generate a following for the festival. Still, no matter how popular he may be with the community and festival visitors, if his productions are sub-standard, the project is in serious trouble. Even if he is both likable and talented in creating stiumlating and attractive Shakespearean stagings, he may have neither business sense nor business manager. That unfortunate combination has wrecked several promising production projects.

Often, all these problems involved in founding, surviving, and eventually excelling converge in that most fundamental problem: subsidy. To some people, the word still has a slightly sinister sound, as in "government subsidies." Champions of free enterprise, for instance, are apt to insist that anything that is really worthwhile will be able to command its proper price in the market place. That has, of course, almost never been true in the arts, among which Shakespearean production must today surely be included. Mass cult entertainment, with its easy, elemental appeals to popular sentiments, sensualities, and biases, has no difficulty in finding a paying public through television, film, and that part of the professional theatre which specializes in farcical comedies and brassy musicals.

But, as William Bowen and William Baumol have pointed out, in *Performing Arts: the Economic Dilemma,* more serious forms of performance are in grave financial danger. Costs of materials, labor, and utilities—not to mention theatre rentals or mortgage payments—have shot up alarmingly in the last two decades and show no signs of being stabilized in the 1970's. Ticket prices cannot be increased on the same scale. Unfortunately, if Shakespeare festivals are to continue to attract audiences, especially from the student and senior citizen sectors where pocket-money is not so plentiful, they cannot escalate admission prices to absorb skyrocketing production costs. Many festivals make a point of cut-rate tickets for school groups, to encourage otherwise reluctant students and teachers to give Shakespeare a try. The two Stratfords, for instance, have developed programs of performances for schools which have extended their seasons. These also give the actors more opportunity to gain experience in their roles, and, it is felt, they are probably building the adult audience of the future, something that must not be neglected, if living theatre is to survive at all. It is too easy to switch on a *free* color TV extravaganza direct from Hollywood, rather than to make the effort of going to the theatre, even when the theatre is nearby and not in Ontario or Connecticut.

That means that winning young audiences and attracting new spectators from among the middle-aged and the seniors must involve the best possible productions at the lowest possible prices. The difference between costs of staging festival programs and maintaining prices of tickets has to be absorbed somehow. Subsidies of various sorts are the answer.

Although subsidy, in the minds of many, is immediately equated with generous monetary gifts—non-repayable—in practice it takes many forms. Some of them are worth more than money to a Shakespeare festival, such as the goodwill of a community which opens its homes to actors and crews for the summer. Other forms of subsidy are not monetary in themselves, but they help to raise money. Having Mrs. George Wallace, the Governor's wife, on its board of directors or attending opening night has been a great help to the Alabama Shakespeare Festival in Anniston. At Odessa, Texas, the 1972 visit of the late Lyndon Johnson and his wife did much to increase the regional prestige of the Globe of the Great Southwest. Ladybird Johnson even loaned a model of her inaugural gown and an oil portrait of the President for lobby display.

Monetary subsidies, of course, do not always involve actual payments into festival coffers. Some of them are accounted for in other budgets. Such festivals as those at the Universities of Vermont, Hofstra, and Colorado, are almost automatically subsidized, in terms of the theatre complexes and shops which are put at their disposal. Sometimes the performers are unpaid students, which is another kind of subsidy. If faculty members direct, design, and operate the technical equipment as part of their normal teaching duties, that too is a subsidy. Costume fabrics, set materials, and special effects may also be purchased out of the annual drama department budget.

In some cases, the only major extra expenses are engaging a visiting director or designer and hiring some professional or semi-professional performers. And the latter costs may often be absorbed as "acting scholarships." College and university-sponsored Shakespeare festivals which are anxious to build a reputation for excellence in production, however, do tend to spend more for their summer shows than for school-year stagings, and they frequently invite well known or promising professionals to work with them as directors, designers, and performers. Such

Universities and colleges serve as the supporting organization for many festivals: The Kansas Shakespeare Festival was supported by the University of Kansas for two summers (right top). The Colorado Shakespeare Festival is a project of the theatre and dance department of the University of Colorado in Boulder (right).

luxuries, however, cost money, and this money is not always to be found in college coffers.

Most festivals—even those with academic sanction and protection—have generous Boards of Trustees, Governors, or Directors. It is the rare festival program which does not contain long lists of Patrons, Sponsors, Benefactors, and Friends. These categories usually indicate the size of the friendship, in terms of dollars donated. In order to pursue public and private subsidy money more effectively, festivals often establish foundations which concern themselves primarily with basic funding and long-range planning.

Festival Friends and Benefactors, of course, often contribute materials and labor, in lieu of cash. In Rochester, New York, for example, a church congregation donated the performance space. But surely the most impressive contribution in recent memory is monetary: the $1 million Mrs. Mitzi E. Newhouse gave Joseph Papp of the New York Shakespeare Festival to launch his initial season of Shakespearean drama and new plays at Lincoln Center. Papp, an aggressive and effective fund-raiser, knows how to say thank-you. He rechristened the Mielziner-Saarinen Forum Theatre as the Mitzi E. Newhouse and designated it the new home of Shakespeare in mid-town Manhattan. If a festival depends heavily on the generosity of a patron—not to mention his leadership in stimulating others to donate—it may find itself in serious difficulties if he dies or defects. With the untimely death in 1974 of Joseph Verner Reed, a founding sponsor of the American Shakespeare Theatre in Stratford, Connecticut, that is exactly what happened. It was reported that Reed had advanced the Theatre $400,000, and the estate quite naturally in the process of settling up called in the notes. That was a blow which the management was able to survive, but it was not so easy to replace Reed's drive and dedication in spearheading fund raising drives.

Subsidy sources from the public sector include the

Two extremes of the subsidy and funding problem are The Stratford Festival of Canada *(top)* which receives generous support from citizens, business, and government, and The Oregon Shakespearean Festival *(above)* which covers 95 percent of its operational costs with box office receipts.

National Endowments for the Arts—for performance aid—and for the Humanities—for training and educational programs—on the federal level in the United States, and across the border, the Canada Council. On the next level, in Canada, the Province of Ontario, the Ontario Council for the Arts, and the Province of Ontario Department of Education provide substantial funding and/or assistance. State councils for the arts perform similar functions for American festivals, but with nothing like the generosity of their Canadian counterparts. County and city arts councils also contribute to festivals in their locality—but not always. Some of the most needy festivals cannot qualify for certain categories of governmental support because their seasons are too short, or their companies too small or non-professional. Corporate and private foundations, as well as corporations, banks, and local businesses, donate to various festival ventures. Sometimes this is an obvious investment, with an eye to developing tourism and its hoped-for influx of dollars. More often it is simply an expression of good will toward the operation, showing an interest in providing a worthwhile community cultural experience.

Private citizens and civic groups, such as the Lions, Rotary, and Kiwanis Clubs, also are important links in the subsidy chain. Lodges and church groups, even school classes, have pooled their donations to help festivals survive and grow.

Money is certainly the most pressing subsidy need. But it is not the only kind of donation gladly accepted by festival managements. Men and women of the community may volunteer their services for technical work such as set construction and costume manufacture. Ticket-selling, ushering, refreshment and souvenir hawking are all jobs which can be filled by local citizens.

Goods like lumber, fabric, old furniture and clothing may also be donated. But printing, advertising, haulage, free rehearsal and storage space, and free or cut-rate utilities may also be made available to the festivals. These visible subsidies, which involve personal commitment to and activity in the festival, are vital in developing a strong sense of community support for such ventures. People who have become involved this way begin to think of the project as "their festival." Opening day Elizabethan banquets help to solidify this feeling, as well as to raise additional money for the season.

Perhaps the most flamboyant—and certainly the most theatrical—example of community support of a Shakespeare festival has been given, appropriately enough, by Los Angeles. Noted stars of TV and film donated their services to help the living theatre by presenting a show in 1973 in the Hollywood Bowl. The benefit performance cleared $20,000 after operating expenses.

Such a talent-show is not only a good way to raise hard cash, but it also focuses attention on the festival's existence. It is invaluable publicity. There are, however, more modest means of providing a publicity subsidy. Over a period of time, they may even prove equally or more effective, thanks to the power of repetition and the cumulative force of volume. It is not unusual for local businesses and industries to use a portion or all of their advertising time and/or space during festival season to help promote the productions. Customarily, they will also buy space in the festival program, making possible its publication with—hopefully—a little extra profit on the side.

One of the most novel but sensible applications of this principle serves the Utah Shakespearean Festival extremely well. The Meadow Gold and Arden Gold Dairies each summer give two out of the four sides on their milk cartons to advertise the Festival. This free commercial reaches south into Arizona and northward as far as Idaho. A portion of the dairies' radio time is also devoted to the Festival.

The Stratford Festival of Canada and the Oregon Shakespearean Festival represent the opposite extremes of subsidy, so it may be interesting to examine them briefly. Since the Ontario Festival's founding in 1953, citizens and businesses in Stratford itself have contributed well over $500,000. This may seem like a lot of money, but it has been spread over two decades. It amounts to an average of $24 for every man, woman, and child in Stratford. When one considers that, according to the Ontario Department of Tourism, more than $8 million—not including the theatre admissions—flows into Stratford every summer season, then it is clear that the inhabitants have made a fantastically profitable investment in Shakespeare. Still, it is well worth noting that this golden hoard does not pour into the Festival treasury, but instead into the pockets of the Stratford citizens. Prosperity for businessmen and for housewives who rent out spare bedrooms to Festival visitors does not necessarily get tithed back into the tourist attraction which made it all possible. Interestingly enough, the prestige generated by the Festival has rubbed off on Stratford, so much so, that since 1953, over 23 new industries have located there, themselves also profiting somewhat from identification with the well known name.

Aside from the contributions from the Stratford community, the Festival has received impressive monetary support from individuals, foundations, corporations, businesses, clubs, and associations. In some cases, it has been a matter of hands-across-the-border, with American foundations, companies, and citizens donating. Some idea of the sums involved may be gained from the receipts of the four major fund drives. In 1953, to launch the first Festival season and erect the tent-theatre, $157,000 was raised. A year later, $141,000 was solicited for working capital and theatre improvements. In 1956, $1,500,000 was generated in a nation-wide appeal, intended to finance construction of a permanent festival theatre. This sum proved $650,000 less than

was actually needed. The balance was obtained with mortgage bonds, retired in 1973. Then, in 1963, in order to buy and adapt the charming old Avon Theatre for expanded Festival performances, $720,000 was raised.

Generous annual operational subsidies for theatres were established early in the 1960's by the Canada Council and the Province of Ontario Council for the Arts. In doing this, Canada took an easy lead over American governmental agencies in supporting the arts. Not only was the Canadian government the first in the arts field, but it came loaded down with handsome subsidies. With such enterprises as the Stratford Festival, the Royal Winnipeg Ballet, Montreal's Theatre du Nouveau Monde, Ottawa's National Ballet, and Toronto's Canadian Opera Company, Canadians demonstrated what talent and subsidy could achieve.

To supplement the governmental subsidies with private and corporate contributions on a more regular basis, in 1966, the Stratford Festival's Board of Governors began annual fund-raising campaigns. The initial target was $100,000. By 1972, the annual intake was some $217,742. The Board raised $220,000 in 1973 and $230,000 in 1974, reflecting the increases in wages and material costs. This money, it must be stressed, is *in addition* to the government subsidies and income from ticket-sales, publications, souvenirs, and refreshments. It makes a $9,000 grant the Texas Arts and Humanities Commission gave the Globe of the Great Southwest, in Odessa, look very puny indeed. True, the Odessa festival is a far more modest operation, but without more public and private support, its modesty may prove embarrassing to prideful Texans.

In the summer of 1970, the Province of Ontario retired 54 percent of the Stratford Festival's accumulated deficit with a single payment. At the same time, the Canada Council paid off one-fifth of the remainder, the first of five annual payments to retire the deficit permanently. Deficits are no longer permitted at the Stratford Festival.

The Stratford Festival has a balanced budget. That means that all the money received as subsidy and earned income is paid out for materials, wages, and services. In the 1974 season, for instance, in addition to the $230,000 raised from patrons and donors, a total of $705,000 was provided from governmental sources. The Canada Council gave $477,000, and its provincial counterpart, the Ontario Council, contributed $228,000. Box office receipts totaled $2,461,500. There was also income from sales of programs, posters, and souvenirs which amounted to $50,000. Although all this adds up to an impressive sum, so do the Festival's operating costs. An Australian tour lost money, in fact, despite a guarantee from Australian authorities. This loss was cheerfully borne, in the belief that such performance junkets enhance the international reputation of the Festival. For recent tours to Russia and Poland, however, the Canadian government covered the expenses. Apparently, it's worth more to officials to impress Slavs in Eastern Europe than Australian cousins. Tours within Canada are also subsidised by the government.

What a contrast then is the Oregon Shakespearean Festival in Ashland! As General Manager Bill Patton says, "It's a difficult subject. When I tell people across the United States—whether they are in university, resident, or festival theatres—that we don't have a subsidy for operation, they look at me with jaundiced eyes.

As if by a wave of Prospero's magic wand, the Rochester Shakespeare Theatre sprang to life in early 1973 with enthusiastic plans to establish a professional resident theatre.

"It is true that we have been able to get the National Endowment for the Arts and the Endowment for the Humanities to cooperate on a grant, along with the Office of Education, to help us in our work with schools. That wasn't a continuing grant unfortunately. As far as the productions are concerned, we are still very much on our own.

"Isolation helped the Festival because we had to be totally practical. If we have any operational subsidy at all, it's in the form of our actors—and volunteers who help in the theatre—but that's true all over the country. We don't get huge sums from large foundations. We don't have a yearly drive to dissolve an operational deficit. Most regional theatres I know of have both grants and deficit drives.'

Since the town of Ashland has a more or less permanent population of 9,000—with some 4,000 college students during the school term—and a median income level of $7,000–$8,000 annually, local deficit drives would not have much hope of raising large sums. It should be remembered that the Canadian Stratford's citizens averaged donations of $24 each *only* after a twenty-year period had passed.

As Patton says, "The Festival had to survive and grow on the basis of whatever operating gain it could make each year over the previous season." In its first year, 1935, the Festival was inaugurated with some WPA money and donations from local merchants. These businessmen lacked the missionary faith of the founder, Professor Angus Bowmer. They insisted that prize-fights be staged in the afternoons, to provide some profit against expected Festival losses. Bowmer reluctantly agreed, rationalizing that Shakespeare's Globe was a stone's throw from a bear-baiting arena. When receipts were tallied, he was pleased and amused to discover that the fights had actually *lost* money, while his Festival venture, in its first season, had not only made its own costs but also could cover the prize-fight deficits, with something to spare for the next year.

Bowmer, whom Patton rightly describes as "very much the optimist and the dreamer," never doubted that his Festival would be an on-going event. The initial season was firmly advertised as "The First Annual Shakespeare Festival." For the second year, what is now Southern Oregon State College replaced the city of Ashland as the sponsor.

The decision was then made to make the Festival a completely separate organization, though amicable cooperation has continued with the college. It was chartered by the State of Oregon as a non-profit educational theatre, but that did not carry with it any kind of state subsidy. From that time to this, it has been governed by a Board of Directors elected from people who had bought memberships, in short, its audience. As Patton explains, "In that sense, the audience really does operate this theatre. They hire the executive staff, the producing director, and the general manager . . . They are by no means puppets, as they are at one well known eastern Shakespeare festival."

At present, however, Ashland is still able to cover about 95 percent of its operational costs from box-office receipts. This must be regarded as phenomenal. Not even the most celebrated European subsidized theatre—let alone any American regional theatre—can boast of such a record. The remaining 5 percent of costs is raised by gifts.

"As far as operations are concerned," Patton stresses, "the only real outside subsidy we have comes from the sale of Festival memberships. All the money that doesn't go into operations is invested in a special trust fund, administered by a separate board. The income goes toward the support of scholarships for actors.

With a 1975 operating budget of nearly $924,000, Patton and his colleagues are to be congratulated on making the books balance primarily through ticket sales. There is almost no support from the state. There was a one-year $9,000 grant from the Oregon

The Rochester Shakespeare Theatre's plan was to use Shakespeare's name and some of his plays as a magnet to draw subscribers. After playing a pilot season in 1973, a full 1973-74 schedule and part of the 1974-75 season, the theatre closed in early December of 1974 because they did not get the local community support and foundation support.

Council on the Arts, to help pay the initial salary of the schools-program coordinator. When it was given, it was the largest arts subsidy ever awarded in Oregon, which certainly points up the contrast with Ontario.

In addition to local support through goods and services, there is another often overlooked source of subsidy for Ashland: the news media. Patton says, "We have never paid for any advertising, and it's another reason we've been able to survive. Television stations from San Francisco to Seattle are giving us thousands of dollars worth of free-time on public service programs. In 1973, we got close to $200,000 worth of free advertising, not counting feature magazine and newspaper articles.

"In 1966, I discovered that the Stratford Festival in Canada was annually spending *more* on media advertising than our entire year's operating budget! I'm not bragging about this. I mention it only as a comparison. We do, of course, provide as many photos, transcriptions, press releases, and other materials as we can; that is our basic advertising expense. As a result, the Festival is very well known on the West Coast and in academic circles. But, if you asked a man on the streets of New York City, he probably would never have heard of us. But then, he probably would not have heard of Stratford, Ontario."

Shakespeare Year-round

American Shakespeare Theatre

It is only a short two hours drive from New York City to the quiet Connecticut town of Stratford, which has been home to the American Shakespeare Festival Theatre since its first season in 1955. The theatre sits on a charming plot of reclaimed marshland which is now green and dotted with huge trees and shaded picnic tables. College students in Elizabethan garb wander about singing madrigals. On fine days, before a performance, the lawn is covered with elegant picnickers and elaborate meals. An evening performance at Stratford seems to bring out linen cloths, candlelight, silver, and bug spray. If nothing else, the American Shakespeare Theatre has become an event—very much a summer activity of nearby New Haven and other Connecticut residents. New Yorkers, too, brave the rush-hour traffic, arriving in time to bolt a quick meal and join an evening of Shakespeare, Shaw, or Wycherley.

Over the years, Festival observers have been disappointed that their satisfaction with the physical setting has not always extended to what is staged inside the wooden-walled, octagonal theatre. From an artistic point of view, the Connecticut Stratford productions have been frequently criticized. But the fact remains that, along with the Ontario Stratford and the New York Shakespeare Festival, the American Shakespeare Theatre is one of the three most professional Shakespeare groups. While a reviewer might be indulgent of regional festivals featuring student actors and educational theatre directors, the Connecticut, Ontario, and New York companies undergo the most probing scrutiny. Any group with their professional claims should. And, it must be pointed out that not one of these three groups emerges untarnished from the drama pages of either *The New York Times* or national magazines.

Since its first season, the American Shakespeare Theatre has had all the right trappings. While none could deny the individual talents of the many big

Stratford, Connecticut 06497
(203) 357–4456
Artistic Director: Michael Kahn

names from the acting, design, and directing fields, the question often was whether or not they lived up to their potential. The last several seasons have indicated that there is a change underway in Connecticut—under the artistic leadership of Michael Kahn. 1974 marked Kahn's eighth season with the Connecticut theatre and his sixth season as artistic director. There have been many hopeful signs that he has taken hold and is setting the theatre on course for more assured and consistent artistic success. One of his great goals—to create a revolving reservoir of actors who would make up the resident company each summer—seems to have been achieved. The theatre could not help but have benefited from that kind of ensemble approach.

Since its first season, the most professional and respected acting talents of Broadway and Hollywood have been spending summers at Stratford. Raymond Massey, Roddy McDowell, Jack Palance, Christopher Plummer, John Colicos, Alfred Drake, Katherine Hepburn, Nancy Marchand, Sada Thompson, Robert Ryan, Douglas Watson, Will Geer, Fritz Weaver, and many more have all taken roles. Designers at the theatre have been creative and ingenious scene-setting artists like Rouben Ter-Arutunian, William Ritman, Ed Wittstein, Douglas Schmidt, and John Conklin. Lighting designers like John Gleason and Marc Weiss have been on hand. Jane Greenwood has been the resident costume designer since 1966. Directors who have been season guests include Word Baker, Douglas Seale, Jerome Kilty, Steven Porter, John Dexter, Peter Gill, Cyril Ritchard, Edward Payson Call, and Edwin Sherin.

With a collection of talents of this calibre, it seems possible that any problems Stratford may

Macbeth *(right)*
Antony and Cleopatra *(below)*
All's Well That Ends Well *(right, below)*

Julius Caesar

Romeo and Juliet

have had, might be blamed on their frequent changes in artistic leadership. It is impossible for a festival to project a consistently good image, regardless of the talents involved, if there is no continuing artistic vision.

For the inaugural 1955 summer, Dennis Carey of the Bristol Old Vic pulled together two productions, *Julius Caesar* and *The Tempest*, with little more than three months' notice. Carey had an almost-finished, $1 million theatre to work in, but no existing acting troupe to work with. John Houseman and Jack Landau led the theatre from 1956 through 1959, when Houseman resigned in a seeming misunderstanding with founder and festival shepherd, Lawrence Langer (formerly the guiding light of the American Theatre Guild). Jack Landau carried on for several years; Allen Fletcher took the helm from the early 1960's until Kahn's arrival.

Founder Lawrence Langer's initial plan was to evolve at Stratford an "American type of Shakespeare presentation." It was to be a year-round operation with a summer festival and a winter of touring plus an acting academy. Only recently has the American Shakespeare Theatre been getting close to the original intent. Winter seasons in 1957, 1958, and 1961 were lackluster, and were dropped until 1969, when that summer's *Henry V* made a brief appearance on Broadway. In 1970, *Othello* followed suit. In 1973, *Macbeth* appeared in the lineup of festive Shakespeare events at the John F. Kennedy Center in Washington. From the 1974 summer season, *Cat on a Hot Tin Roof* moved on to Broadway. The projected acting academy seems never to have gotten beyond the groups of fellowship students and journeymen that join each summer's acting company. Faced with financial difficulties in 1974, the fellowship program was terminated—with hopes that it might be reinstituted in the future.

Experimental plays and playwrights are a relatively new addition to the Stratford activities. In 1971, the Festival introduced an experimental New Playwrights Series. It is devoted to producing new plays by promising playwrights, in a workshop situation. Generally the program consists of four plays by four different writers, and most of the company's actors and directors get involved in some capacity.

Perhaps the most successful continuing operation at the American Shakespeare Theatre is the activity of the Education Department, carried out under the watchful eye of Mary Hunter Wolf. The education department does more than provide standard program publications, and teacher preparations. The Center for Theatre Techniques in Education has been working in two major areas: the teaching of drama as theatre, and the use of improvisation and theatre games as a way to create better classroom learning atmosphere. This program is enthusiastically supported by a number of federal, state, and private foundation grants.

In addition, each summer, under the direction of Allen Lewis, the nearby University of Bridgeport sponsors (in co-operation with the theatre) a Shakespeare Institute for graduate study that is open to teachers, students, and university theatre directors. The theatre has also sponsored annual weekend seminars consisting of productions and discussions in conjunction with regional theatre associations.

But, by far the most popular venture of theAmerican Shakespeare Theatre is their season of student programs. Each spring, preceding the mid-June to early-September season, the theatre has staged a ten to eleven-week student audience season. The plays are previews for the summer shows or hold-overs from the last season. Contributions from their theatre guild allows ticket prices to be cut to $3 for the students. The annual audience of over 120,000 is bussed in from all over the Northeastern region. Some come from as far away as the Midwest and the

the South. The theatre has even organized charter flights and motel plans for longer school trips. In 1972, while the summer season played to only 68% capacity, the audiences at the student series filled 96% of the house. The two most outstanding drawbacks of the theatre building are magnified to a maddening degree during this season. Faced with the theatre's poor sightlines, students must squirm to see, then the always-irritating squeaking of the theatre seats comes close to drowning out the Bard's blank verse entirely.

Costumes and scenery for the American Shakespeare Theatre are a visual delight. For recent summer seasons, one lighting designer, Marc Weiss, has been in residence for all the shows. Resident costumer Jane Greenwood has been designing each show and carefully tending to its execution at New York costume house Brooks Van Horn. To stretch the budget as far as possible, Greenwood's costumes join the Brooks Van Horn rentable stock after their Connecticut season. Some summer programs such as the 1972 season of *Julius Casear* and *Antony and Cleopatra* allow for costumes to overlap from one production to the next. The theatre has been experimenting with different scenic design solutions. Some years they have hired a different designer for each show; other years as in 1974, one designer, in this case John Conklin, is in residence for the whole season. In 1972, Robin Wagner designed both of the Roman plays. On the other hand in 1973, Ed Wittstein designed *The Country Wife*, while William Ritman created a clever, multi-use unit set for *Measure for Measure*, and Douglas Schmidt created a much talked about stainless steel vision of Macbeth's Scotland. And, in 1974 John Conklin designed the entire season: *Twelfth Night, Romeo and Juliet* and *Cat on a Hot Tin Roof*.

In recent seasons, the American Shakespeare Theatre has been diversifying its play selection so

The Tempest *(above)*
Antony and Cleopatra *(facing page, top)*
Othello *(facing page, bottom)*

that at least one non-Shakespeare play is included in each season. Shaw's *Devil's Disciple* and *Major Barbara* have both appeared; Wycherley's *The Country Wife* in the 1973 season was the theatre's first try at Restoration comedy. The 1974 selection of Tennessee Williams' *Cat on a Hot Tin Roof* demonstrates an unusual willingness on the part of a Shakespeare theatre to present a modern play.

At the close of the 1973 season the theatre was projecting expansion into a four-play season as well as reviving the winter touring plan—with Washington, D.C., Philadelphia, Los Angeles, San Francisco, Chicago, Dallas, Baltimore, and Detroit mentioned as possible stops. They were thinking about a mid-winter residence at a university; expanding the New Playwrights Series; and improving their buildings. But inflation, reticent funding from arts organizations, the untimely death of their president, Joseph Verner Reed, which resulted in the unexpected repayment of a loan to his estate, have all combined to create financial difficulties for the theatre. They estimate that about $300,000 was cut from their budget—which spelled the end of the fellowship program, the curtailment of the student series, and economies at all production levels.

Michael Kahn is currently artistic director of the McCarter Theatre at Princeton. Holding one winter and one summer position, Kahn is able to develop new talents as well as employ many of his company of actors year-round.

Perhaps the most symbolic occurrence of the last two seasons was the theatre's recent name change. Long known as the American Shakespeare Festival Theatre, the group dropped the "Festival." As such and under Kahn's continuing direction, the theatre is moving away from summer festival games and into the serious year-round development of an American Shakespeare Theatre.

Folger
Theatre
Group

Folger Shakespeare Library
201 East Capitol Street
Washington, D.C. 20003
. (202) 547–3230
Producing Director: Louis Scheeder

Encased in the Folger Shakespeare Library—one of Washington's many official-looking buildings—is a charming 200-seat Elizabethan theatre. It is not a replica of any particular theatre—neither the Globe nor the Swan—some think it is most like the Fortune. Since its inauguration in the 1930's, the Folger Shakespeare Library has become a major seat of Shakespearean studies in the United States—and maybe in the world. But it is one of those paradoxes that the Folger Theatre never became a home to an active Shakespeare Festival. Indeed, until 1970, the theatre was virtually unused—except for one production of *Julius Caesar* during the 1940's. Fire department regulations made it impossible to perform regularly in the beautifully painted, wooden room. It is also not hard to imagine that scholars and academicians, as well as the trustees of Amherst College, who administer the Folger Shakespeare Library, were just as pleased not to see the peace and calm of their Reading Room disturbed by theatre folk.

But in 1970, a new director, O. B . Hardison, took over the Library and a young Virginian, Richmond Crinkely, managed to convince the trustees that he could be trusted with the Elizabethan theatre. Since that first season the Folger Theatre Group has become an exciting and vital force in the area—frequently they are referred to as the Off–Broadway of Washington—indeed several of their productions have moved to New York's Off-Broadway.

In setting a direction for the Folger Theatre Group, Richmond Crinkley was too astute and too creative a theatre person to fall into the obvious trap of that mecca of Shakespearean scholars. Perfect-in-every-detail Shakespeare would never entirely satisfy the scholars and would probably bore both audience and critics. Instead, the four play season concentrates on contemporary plays—ones that have for today's audiences perhaps the same impact that Shakespeare's did on the Elizabethans. The Group's commitment

Henry IV, Part I *(left and above)*

to the Library requires that they produce two classic and two new plays each season. Working under an agreement with Actors' Equity which allows them to hire up to five Equity guest artists, at least one of those classics is a Shakespeare—usually timed to celebrate the Bard's birthday. Although in other years, it is not unlikely that the Group might prefer to stage two Shakespeares—as they did in 1974–75 with *Henry IV, Part I* and *The Tempest.* Under Crinkley, the Folger's contemporary play production included the premier of Percy Granger's *The Complete Works of Studs Edsel* and the American premier of Christopher Hampton's *Total Eclipse.*

Crinkley's creative approach at the Folger was so admired by Roger L. Stevens, chairman of the Kennedy Center of the Performing Arts, that he took Crinkley on as an assistant. Former associate producer Louis Scheeder moved into the producer's slot, and the Folger 1973–74 season began with the American premier of *Creeps* by David Freeman—it is an eye-averting look into the world of a cerebral palsy worksheiter. The American premier of an Edinburgh Festival play—*Edward G., Like the Film Star*—and Gogol's *Inspector General* completed the season. The Bard's birthday play was *Love's Labour's Lost*—a musical adaptation commissioned for the Folger on a $10,000 grant from the Eugene and Agnes E. Meyer Foundation. In 1974–75, the two new plays were the American premier of David Storey's *The Farm* and *He's Got A Jones* by new playwright, G. Tito Shaw.

Staging Shakespeare with Elizabethan accuracy is not always a major concern of the Folger Theatre Group. Their *Twelfth Night* in 1971 was a geodesic, mylar dome vision; 1972's *Romeo and Juliet* placed the lovers in rival circus families, and the 1973 *Winter's Tale* was done on the bare, carpeted stage in modern dress. In 1974, *Love's Labour's Lost* was presented with white walls, umbrellas and ladders replacing the traditional forests, while their *Henry IV, Part I* masked the theatre's walls with stone and costumed in more traditional interpretation.

During the initial building construction, Shakespearean collector Henry Clay Folger's instructions to his library achitect, Paul Cret, were to create an "evocation" of an Elizabethan theatre. The theatre's permanent architectural stage house is predictably two-leveled, providing acting space on the stage in front of the first level, and in the second floor's inner room, and from balcony windows. There are also minimal flying facilities through the "heavens," a trap door in the stage house ceiling. The set shop is at this upper level and all built scenery has to be lowered through the "heavens." Folger also stipulated that there be some set storage space, dressing rooms, and lighting controls. It was obvious that Folger intended the theatre to be used. All that was needed after the 1970 approval was for the theatre structure to be fireproofed. The Library staff still lives in constant dread that something in the theatre shops will start a fire that might spread to the valuable collection. Before the first performance, the stage was extended over the first two rows of seats to form a modified thrust and give more acting space on the tiny stage.

The Folger Theatre Group has experimented with various ways of handling the stage and costume design. Costumes are sometimes designed and built especially for the Folger production and other times rented. They have not gone to great lengths to maintain the "integrity" of the Elizabethan stage house: sometimes they mask it with an entirely different setting, other times the half-timbered façade forms virtually the only scenery. The Group has tried hiring designers to be in residence for a whole season. In 1973–74 one designer, David Chapman, was hired as a consultant to do several shows and oversee the rest. In 1974–75, the more diversified design teams

Elizabethan Theatre of the Folger Shakespeare Library,
home of the Folger Theatre Group

Love's Labour's Lost *(left)*
Twelfth Night *(left, below)*
Henry IV, Part I *(below)*

Romeo and Juliet
(*left and below*)

included for *Henry IV, Part I,* William Mickley (sets), Joan Theil (costumes) and Arden Fingerhut (lights), and for *The Tempest,* Stuart Wurtzel (sets), Joan Theil (costumes) and Betsy Toth (lights).

A normal year at the Folger Theatre Group sees four shows on stage. They have recently air conditioned the space so that it is now possible to extend their season into the summer and play all year. The company's 638 subscriptions for the 1973–74 season jumped to 2300 in 1974–75—a definite indication of their acceptance in the Washington area. Company manager Ray Hanley estimates their annual production budget to be currently running about $120,000. Combining that figure with their administrative and operational costs means that the Folger is a deficit operation with one-third of their costs covered by box office receipts and the rest of the tab and some special events being covered by foundations. The group has received generous assistance from the National Endowment for the Arts, the D.C. Commission on the Arts and Humanities, the Marcus and Harryette Cohn Foundation and the Eugene and Agnes E. Meyer Foundation. A grant from the C.B.S. Foundation enabled the group to purchase new theatre seating and a grant from the Morris and Gwendolyn Cafritz Foundation supported the production of *Bartholomew Fair* in honor of Ben Jonson's 400th birthday.

In an elegant little Elizabethan setting, surrounded by mountains of Shakespearean studies, the Folger Theatre Group is paying homage to the Bard more by a forward-looking concern with modern English language playwrights than a tradition-bound dwelling on the first great playwright of the English language.

New York Shakespeare Festival

In 1973 at ceremonies marking the official opening of Lincoln Center's Vivian Beaumont Theatre under producer Joseph Papp's newly installed regime, New York's outgoing mayor, John Lindsay, commented, "I am only sorry Joe Papp isn't running for Mayor. He deserves the job."

To many people it seemed clear that Joseph Papp had already been serving as Mayor—at least for the theatre community. There was no getting around the fact that in the country's theatre capital, Joseph Papp's organization had a monopoly on most of what was new, talked-about, and exciting during seasons of Broadway lethargy, dwindling audience, and general disenchantment with all theatrical enterprises. And, all this activity started with a Shakespeare Festival—one that has served as a model for many other cities' Shakespearean ventures.

From the New York Shakespeare Festival acorn has grown a mighty theatre oak with roots in the Public Theatre (downtown), the outdoor Delacorte Theatre in Central Park, and most recently in Lincoln Center. Nor should the mobile theatre, which tours summer festival productions to the city parks, be forgotten. Papp has even tried his hand at publishing: a monthly magazine of new plays, *Scripts,* is now defunct, and *Performance,* cast in *The Drama Review* image, was banished by Papp and has since suspended publication.

It began to look like a monopoly. It felt like one, too. But, without the New York Shakespeare Festival's Public Theatre, Delacorte Theatre, or Lincoln Center, it was hard to imagine why New York audiences would have gone to the theatre.

Joseph Papp carries out his producing activities with all the pugnacious energy of a street-fighter. Certainly he has made enemies. All men with his success and the abilities to use his successes, have done so. There are rejected playwrights, overlooked actors and directors, and envious producers all hop-

425 Lafayette Street
New York, New York 10003
Delacorte box office (212) 535–5630
Public Theatre: 677–6350

Producer: Joseph Papp

ing to see Papp fail. Certainly, he has had his share of unsuccessful productions and disjointed seasons.

1971, 1972, and 1973 were very big years for Joseph Papp and associate producer Bernard Gersten. A number of their productions that opened at the Delacorte or the Public Theatre moved to Broadway or to television, won Tony awards and Pulitzer prizes. The rock musical *Two Gentlemen of Verona* moved to Broadway from the Park. Jason Miller's *That Championship Season* and David Rabe's *Sticks and Bones* both moved from the Public Theatre to prize-winning Broadway runs. *Much Ado About Nothing* moved from the Park, not only to Broadway, but also on to the television screen. *Sticks and Bones,* also filmed for television, became the focus of a now-famous dispute about television network censorship, but after the Vietnam prisoner-return, the show was eventually televised.

In the many adulatory words frequently written about the Shakespeare Festival enterprises, it was not often noted that while all the hurrahs were taking place on Broadway and in TV rooms around the country, there were no new, widely acclaimed successes at either the Public Theatre during the 1972–73 season, nor in Central Park during the summer of 1973—although a *King Lear* starring James Earl Jones was filmed for WNET'S *Theatre in America* series.

Obviously undaunted, Joseph Papp practically leapt at the opportunity to move into the Lincoln Center theatre left vacant by Jules Irving's failing and departing Lincoln Center Repertory Company. And with a typical spurt of energy, Papp drummed up a spectacular $1 million gift from Mitzi Newhouse, grants from the Ford Foundation, and others in order to launch his first season in the new home. The Eero Saarinen–Jo Mielziner–designed Vivian Beaumont Theatre was slightly redesigned to lower the lighting grid and provide some different seating,

Henry VI, Part I

and a season of plays began. Meanwhile at the newly renamed Mitzi E. Newhouse Theatre (formerly the Forum), in what is probably the most jewel-like house for Shakespeare production in the country, Papp embarked on a winter season of Shakespeare to complement the summers in Central Park.

Nor in all the excitement over the Lincoln Center opening was the downtown Public Theatre being overlooked: a season of new plays was planned and of course there will always be a season of at least two Shakespeare plays at the outdoor Delacorte— free to anyone who stands in line early enough and long enough to get tickets. After all, it was free Shakespeare that launched Joseph Papp into his producing empire.

In 1953, Joseph Papp was a CBS-TV stage-manager with a long standing love of Shakespeare and some experience staging shows for the Navy, plus more experience with the West Coast Actor's Laboratory. He put together a Shakespeare workshop which performed first in a Lower East Side New York church, then in an amphitheatre in East River Park, and finally moved to a truck stage in Central Park.

After Papp's run-ins with the city government and, in particular, the Parks Commissioner who complained that the free Shakespeare audience was trampling the park's crab grass, publisher George Delacorte donated $150,000 toward the completion of the new outdoor Central Park theatre, which opened its gates to non-paying audience members in the summer of 1961. By 1964, a new mobile theatre had been put together out of a series of 5 trailer trucks—housing dressing rooms, bleacher seating, lighting equipment, and a portable stage unit which unfolds from one side of a 40-foot trailer bed. Each summer a production (usually one that appeared on the Central Park stage) appears in the parks of New York's five boroughs.

By 1967, with their commitment to the production of the Bard firmly under control, the group moved into the former Astor Library and began expanding production work into new as well as classical plays. At the time Papp commented, "We are turning to contemporary drama not because of a surfeit with Shakespeare but because of the challenge posed by new audiences we have reached and the need to give dramatic expression to the thinking of our time."

The Astor Library was remodelled and renovated into the Public Theatre complex, which has produced the plays of more than 40 new American playwrights. The Public Theatre houses administrative offices, costume, set, and props shops, art gallery space, and a 300-seat thrust stage, the Florence Anspacher Theatre; a 300-seat end stage, the Estelle R. Newman Theatre; the open flexible staging area of Martinson Hall, and a small 100-seat space called the Other Stage. Across the street is the Public Theatre annex.

The transition from library to permanent theatre has not been without its difficulties—financial and otherwise. One summer, in the face of cancellation of free Shakespeare, Papp staged an all-night, marathon *Wars of the Roses (Henry VI, Parts I and II,* and *Richard III)* to bring attention and funding. The downtown Astor Library was purchased by Papp in 1966 for $575,000. Eventually the city of New York bought the landmark building back for $2.6 million to help the Public Theatre out of debts accumulated for mortgages, renovation, and to provide operating expenses. The Festival now leases the building back from the city at $1 a year.

Despite the burgeoning size of the New York Shakespeare Festival operations—whether they are performing in the Mobile Theatre unit, the Delacorte, the Public Theatre's many stages, or the two Lincoln Center theatres—there is a strong repertory feeling about the Festival productions. There is a solid core of actors that appear again and again. Some, like Raul Julia, Charles Durning, Tom Aldredge, Douglas Watson, seem to work frequently for the Festival. Other actors like James Earl Jones, Coleen Dewhurst, Julie Harris show up regularly in Festival productions.

Papp has a stable of both directors and playwrights in whose work and careers he takes a paternalistic interest. He seems intent on fostering an atmosphere for exploring the theatrical possibilities of new plays and old. The same repertory quality extends into the design aspects of the many New York Shakespeare Festival productions. Theoni Aldredge has been the principal costume designer since 1960, and Martin Aronstein is almost solely responsible for the lighting design. Ming Cho Lee lent his scenic artistry to the Festival from 1962 through 1972. In the summer of 1973, Santo Loquasto was responsible for the Delacorte Theatre designs, and moved on to oversee the reshaping of the Vivian Beaumont Theatre, plus the design of many Lincoln Center productions. As production work proliferated, a number of other set, costume, and lighting designers have been working for the Festival.

Joseph Papp seems to be somewhat of a magician at rounding up funding for his various enterprises. Florence Anspacher, Estelle Newman, Mitzi Newhouse, the Martinsons, and George Delacorte have all been memorialized for their financial assistance. The Festival honor roll of benefactors, donors, founders, and patrons is a healthy cross-section of individuals, private foundations, and union supporters, not to mention state and federal agencies. To launch his new Lincoln Center, Papp received, in addition to the Mitzi Newhouse $1 million, $1.5 mil-

Pericles on New York's Central Park stage

Macbeth *(right)* staged at the
Mitzi E. Newhouse Theatre in Lincoln Center

Much Ado About Nothing *(far right)*
Hamlet *(below)* at the outdoor Delacorte Theatre

lion from the Ford Foundation, $350,000 from the Rockefeller Foundation, $100,000 from the Mellon Foundation, and $50,000 from I.B.M.

At the time that the New York Shakespeare Festival expanded its operations to encompass Lincoln Center, there was some question as to whether the widespread operations would dilute the impact of the Public Theatre's work. At the close of their second season in Lincoln Center, the answer would seem to be: no, not dilute, but certainly change. During the first season both the Vivian Beaumont and the Newhouse Theatres' announced schedules were changed, rearranged, and augmented. Much of the contemporary playwright work that had been done at the Public Theatre was brought uptown. Not all the critics, nor for that matter the subscription audiences, were enthusiastic about what confronted them in a theatre they had come to think of as a safe, classical production house. In 1973–1974, David Rabe's *Boom Boom Room,* Hugh Leonard's *The Au Pair Man,* Ron Milner's *What the Wine Sellers Buy* and Strindberg's *Dance of Death* met with mixed receptions. The season's generally acclaimed "hit" was Miguel Pinero's *Short Eyes*—a production that moved uptown from the Public Theatre. In the downstairs Newhouse, *Troilus and Cressida, The Tempest,* and *Macbeth* were staged to less than enthusiastic critical response, and in fact *Macbeth* never officially opened for critics. During the summer *Pericles* and *Merry Wives of Windsor* were staged in the Park as the Festival's plans to build a new theatre to replace the Delacorte were stirring up controversy at the Parks Department, with the director of preservation and restoration, and in the newspapers. The plan has since been shelved.

Predictably and characteristically, the 1974–75 season has stirred up controversy, sometimes distaste (Anne Burr's *Mert and Phil)* as well as raves—glowing ones for Liv Ullman in *Doll's House.*

Shakespearean work in the Newhouse has been lethargic, many suspect the Bard is now far down on the Festival's list of year-round priorities. Downtown, with much of the new playwright production effort being directed to the Lincoln Center Theatre, the many spaces of the Public Theatre are filled with workshops—frequently not officially opened—and Joseph Papp productions of other theatre companies' works, in addition to the Public Theatre's own productions of new plays not selected for the uptown season. In what appears a major policy shift, Papp announced in March of 1974 that the Lincoln Center subscription season would henceforth concentrate on "big-name" stars in classical plays.

In talking about the New York Shakespeare Festival, one always ends up dealing directly with one man—Joseph Papp. He may not always be admired for his methods. In fact, he seems to thrive on the controversy he stirs up in city council budget hearings, with drama critics whom he berates when his productions are criticised, and with certain regional theatre leaders. But, nonetheless, Papp has to be admired—and thanked—for what he has achieved both for the production of new playwrights' works, as well as those of William Shakespeare. Not long ago *New Yorker* magazine published a cartoon in which radiating over the skyline of New York were the bold words: *A Joseph Papp Production.* And that's the way it has seemed.

Odessa Shakespeare Festival

The Globe of the Great Southwest
2308 Shakespeare Road
Odessa, Texas 79761
(915) 332–4031
Producing Director: Charles McCally

A Chekhov or a Gorky Festival might seem more appropriate than a Shakespeare Festival to a city bearing the historic name of Odessa. In fact, even though the Odessa Shakespeare Festival is located in West Texas, rather than on the Crimean Sea, this city's earliest associations are Russian. First settled by Russian Baptist emigrants, the community took its name from its East European namesake, primarily owing to a similarity of terrain.

Today there are no strongly visible reminders of this Russian influence in Odessa. And, aside from the many evidences of an active role in Texas oil production, the city's most impressive physical feature is now its Old Globe of the Great Southwest. Each summer since its inauguration in 1968, this unique theatre has been the scene of a play season featuring two dramas by William Shakespeare, plus a third, sometimes a classic from the world theatre repertoire. Beginning in late June and running until late August, the performances attract people from all over Texas and from neighboring states as well. Odessa's Shakespeare adventure began in an odd way. In 1948, so the story goes, Mrs. Marjorie Morris noted that it would be interesting to see *Macbeth* acted on a replica of the stage where it was first performed. She was teaching a Senior English class at the Odessa High School. One of the students had made a model of the Globe, based on published scholarly speculations. The idea took root in Mrs. Morris' mind. She saw no reason why students should not see *Macbeth* in an Elizabethan theatre reconstruction; she also became convinced that·that is exactly what they should be able to do.

Initial interest in the project burned bright, only to die down when Mrs. Morris left Odessa to earn an M.A. Her thesis title: *The Proposed Globe Theatre at Odessa, Texas.* On her return, armed with her thesis and extensive plans by J. Ellsworth Powell, Mrs. Morris began teaching at Odessa College. She rallied a group of local citizens to collect funds for the Globe-to-be. In 1958, a down payment was made for the project, planned for a triangular strip of land adjacent to the college campus. Wisely, Mrs. Morris saw to it that the theatre and its activities would be independent from the College.

After Mrs. Morris's Globe was completed, there was some question of how it might be used. It was christened to the service of Shakespeare by a *Kiss Me, Kate!* production, prepared by the Permian Playhouse, a local community theatre troupe. Then Paul Baker's Dallas Theatre Group brought a professional mounting of *Julius Caesar* to its boards. In 1969, Charles David McCally, a professional actor and director, was hired as producer-director. McCally, a tall Texan who had performed with Eva Le Gallienne and the National Repertory Theatre as well as with Paul Baker's players, was asked to create not only a Shakespeare Festival, but also a year-round semi-professional regional theatre program. This he has done.

The 1974 Globe year featured the musical *Oklahoma!* and a Theatre of the Absurd program in the spring. The latter was a bill of Ionesco's *The Bald Soprano* and Albee's *The Sandbox.* Summer Shakespeare productions were *Macbeth,* staged by McCally, and *Twelfth Night,* directed by actress Clare Luce, a frequent guest artist at the Globe. The program was rounded out with Moliere's *Imaginary Invalid,* another McCally mounting. Fall was highlighted with the world premier of a film on Shakespeare, *All the World's a Stage.* Scripted by Arlene Momeyer and Walter Buck, this film was made with the Odessa Shakespeare performers. Another premier in November 1974 was a new play by Regina McCally, *George's Jean,* a drama about critic George Jean Nathan and Julie Haydon. For 1975's summer program, Charles McCally scheduled *Much Ado About Nothing* and *Troilus and Cressida,* comple-

The Globe of the Great Southwest exterior *(top)* and interior Tiring House *(bottom)*

The Merchant of Venice *(top)*
A Midsummer Night's Dream *(bottom)*

mented by the musical, *Dames at Sea,* and a drama on the life of Christ, for special Sunday performances.

In 1970, McCally and his ensemble toured England's Lake District with their special adaptations of *Hamlet* and *The World of Carl Sandburg.* These were well received by British reviewers and spectators. Back home in Odessa, the reviews also tend to be admiring, and McCally has a file of appreciative quotes not only from major Texas newspaper critics, but also from national reviewers. Among them are flattering comments from *Life* magazine, the *New York Times,* and the *Saturday Review,* whose Henry Hewes has strongly supported the Globe's work.

McCally, as producer and director, is trying to make Shakespeare viable for West Texas audiences. His Western *Shrew* is a fairly successful attempt, though the concept is not entirely a new one. At present, he has certain difficulties to cope with, in trying to achieve productions which will be worthy of their hallowed texts and of sufficient professional quality to reward those who may come great distances for the Odessa plays. In its first season, for example, visitors from forty states and fifteen foreign countries were recorded in the Festival Guest Book. Naturally, neither McCally nor his enthusiastic Board of Governors wants to disappoint their expectations. Yet, one of those governors seemed rather proud as he announced in the early 1970's, that the Board had imposed a two-hour limitation. No production of the Bard's masterpieces could last longer than two hours, on the premise that this is a good way to build Texas tolerance to Shakespeare gradually. Over the summers, the performance time can be extended. The Odessa Festival must have what is surely one of the smallest American subsidies, despite the fabled wealth of Odessa's principal inhabitants. In 1972, members of the Texas Arts and Humanities Commission visited a performance of *Shrew.* They seemed quite pleased with a gift they had brought: a check for $9,000 to help defray production costs. Compared with the subsidies and donations which make the New York Shakespeare Festival, the American Shakespeare Theatre, and the Stratford Festival of Canada possible, such a grant was—while welcome, and even desperately needed—still pathetically inadequate.

Thanks to ties with the University of Texas of the Permian Basin, the Festival now looks for some of its young performers at the University Resident Theatre Association auditions. When and where possible, McCally uses seasoned professionals, but this depends more on funds than on performer availability.

In the early years of the 1970's, nearly twenty people were on salary, with five or six Odessans performing or helping out for the experience they gained. $75 was top, scaled down to $50, with housing provided by the Festival. The ensemble had to buy its own meals out of wages. Low salaries don't seem to bother McCally's actors. The chance to perform in an Elizabethan theatre and to interpret major Bardic roles are the real magnets. But then, McCally points out, ". . . when they arrive and discover that their part—this famous role that they've always wanted to do—has been cut down to a G-String, they're pretty unhappy."

The theatre is intimate and attractive. It is advertised as "the world's most authentic replica of Shakespeare's 16th Century English Theatre," and also as "the world's only faithful replica . . ." Since Shakespeare's Globe was at least partially open to the elements and Odessa's is completely covered, these claims cannot be sustained on that ground alone. There are other rather shaky grounds as well. Nonetheless, the octagonal house, with its 418 seats, 30' by 60' thrust stage, "Elizabethan Tiring House," and bogus Tudor decor is a pleasant and fairly practical theatre milieu.

The Taming of the Shrew

Oregon Shakespearean Festival

P.O. Box 605
Ashland, Oregon 97520
(503) 482–2111 or 482–4331 (Box Office)
Producing Director: Jerry Turner

Ashland's Shakespeare Festival is about as far removed from the center of America's professional theatre activity—New York City—as performing artists can get, short of building a Globe Theatre on Oahu. It doesn't receive the generous publicity given to the Shakespeare Theatre in Connecticut's Stratford. Nor does it receive the impressive government subsidies and private donations which have helped Canada's Stratford Festival to prosper.

Yet considering the quality of its productions and the dynamism of its ensemble enthusiasm, in recent years its work has been worthy of comparison with these two well known Shakespeare ventures. At first glance, that might not seem so remarkable. Both the Stratfords are thoroughly professional operations, and there is no reason why an equally professional festival could not develop in Oregon's Rogue River Valley, given talent, money, and audiences.

Those three important variables are what distinguish the Ashland adventure and make its success so impressive. Most of the talent involved in this Festival is not yet professional, though the performances are often more skillful than those of Equity actors at some other Shakespeare seasons. The production company of about 160 members is selected, via audition and recommendation, from all over the United States. Most of the predominantly young performers are given scholarships. A few may work without pay, simply to gain experience in acting and theatre crafts. Usually the ensemble and part of the staff are drawn from the students, faculty, and technical experts of America's major university drama departments. This is so well established now that some of the company are able to get undergraduate and graduate credits for Ashland activities. The year-round artistic, administrative, and technical chiefs and their assistants are, however, seasoned theatre professionals.

The combination of the eagerness and ability of

Troilus and Cressida

The Taming of the Shrew *(above)*
Love's Labour's Lost *(far left)*
Hamlet *(left)*

the relatively inexperienced performers with the innovative and fairly disciplined production approach of the Festival management seems to be the formula for Ashland's polish and apparent professionalism. It is a combination which is drawing increasingly large audiences to this summer festival. And, as a result, the season has gradually grown in length, breadth, and depth, making it a cultural phenomenon on the West Coast.

Shakespeare is not often associated with the Fourth of July, but that date marks his first territorial claim in Oregon. In 1935, Professor Angus L. Bowmer, of the Southern Oregon College faculty, founded the festival as part of a Fourth of July celebration. He never lacked confidence in the venture. This is indicated by the title he gave to it: "The First Annual Shakespeare Festival." In 1975, he found himself more than vindicated with the festival in its 35th season. If 35 and 35 don't add up to 75, it is because the original festival theatre was damaged by fire in 1940. By 1941, World War II put severe limitations on availability of actors, materials, and gasoline for the cars of festival visitors. Production was halted until 1947, when the Festival re-opened with the dedication of a new theatre. Bowmer's intent had always been to present Shakespeare's works in an arena as much like that used by Shakespeare as possible. Given the scholarly uncertainties about the actual structure of the Globe Theatre, he had his new theatre design based on the 1599 Fortune Theatre contract specifications. But neither that theatre nor the one which replaced it in 1959—the third on that site—were dubbed either "Globe" or "Fortune." Then as now, it was simply identified as "America's First Elizabethan Theatre." Bowmer and his colleagues are justly proud that theirs is also America's first and oldest surviving Shakespeare Festival.

Each year in the Festival's performing history marks some interesting development: an extension of the season, the addition of new equipment, the creation of some special adjunct program, the inauguration of a new theatre. In 1953, the season was expanded to fill the entire month of August. By 1963, the Festival offered a season of 46 nights. With two theatres in 1973, there were 164 performances, spreading from mid-June to early September. The outdoor Elizabethan Theatre played to a nightly average of 99.3 percent of its capacity of 1,194 seats. This is success with a vengeance. It is the kind of success which effectually *forced* the Oregon Shakespearean Festival Association to build the modern, handsome, comfortable, indoor Angus Bowmer Theatre, dedicated in 1970.

In the 1950's and the early 1960's, it was still possible for Bardolators to drive up the California Coast from Los Angeles, Santa Barbara, or San Francisco, enjoying the redwood forests on the way, and arrive in Ashland where they could buy tickets on the day of performance. After 1965, however, more and more theatre tourists found that the Elizabethan Theatre was completely sold out, often weeks ahead of time. To be able to absorb the growing audience, to stay flexible, the Bowmer was constructed.

In Ashland B. B.—or Before the Bowmer—the Festival slogan was "Stay Four Days—See Four Plays." Those banners still flutter from town lamp-posts today, but a more accurate motto would be: "Stay *Three* Days—See *Six* Plays." Now, instead of four dramas in the Elizabethan Theatre, there are three Shakespeare plays, making possible greater audience turnover in that arena. And the Bowmer also offers three productions, one of them customarily indoor Shakespeare, with the remaining two being venerable or modern classics, such as *The Alchemist, Uncle Vanya, The Crucible,* and *The Dance of Death.*

Outdoor Shakespeare is always performed at night, just as the sun is beginning to disappear be-

The Oregon Shakespeare Festival's outdoor Elizabethan Theatre *(left)*; stagehouse set for Love's Labour's Lost *(far left)* and during performance *(below)*

hind the Siskyiou Mountains, which shelter Ashland and the theatre-complex at their feet. Since Bowmer has always insisted that the Bard's plays be performed as completely as possible, each show runs some three hours or more, without intermission. The indoor Bowmer Theatre shows are always matinees during the summer season, but some Ashland drama tourists, much as they admire the productions, prefer to stay six days to see the plays. Five to six hours of high drama three days in a row, especially when it is performed with skill and power, require real dedication. Staying six days requires as much advance planning as obtaining tickets now. Although a number of modern motels have sprung up in and around Ashland, accommodations are at a premium the entire summer. Some visitors find they must stay in Medford, a short distance from Ashland.

Among memorable recent productions in the Elizabethan Theatre have been the 1972 *Taming of the Shrew,* directed by Robert Benedetti, and *Love's Labour's Lost,* staged by Laird Williamson. In 1973, Pat Patton's mounting of *As You Like It* was as charming and professional as any production of Shakespearean comedy to be seen at the major East Coast festivals. Laird Williamson's vision of *Henry V* was also impressive. Although like all the Shakespeare canon staged in the Elizabethan Theatre, it stressed period costume and effective use of the various levels of the stage, Williamson was able to innovate imaginatively without harming the Elizabethan texture. This was notable in a strongly choreographed Battle of Agincourt sequence.

In the Bowmer Theatre, more experimentation is possible. A recent *Troilus and Cressida* had a strikingly modern setting, by Festival designer Richard Hay, which evoked the daring scenic and lighting experiments of the late Wieland Wagner at Bayreuth. Hay's visualization of Arthur Miller's *The Crucible*—in a starkly limited palette of blacks, greys, and whites—also made the impact of this strongly performed, simply designed production very great.

As with Bowmer, who is now the Festival's development consultant, Hay's continuity of design work has contributed much to the visual consistency and integrity of Ashland's work. Although both the Elizabethan Theatre and the Bowmer Theatre were given their final blueprint form by professional architects, it was Hay who made the initial design suggestions for these ingeniously devised playhouses. One theatre is intended to belong, spiritually at least, to the Elizabethan period; the other is of the modern world modern. And yet, in colors, materials, textures, and simple elements of line, angle, and curve, they complement each other very well. They also share a backstage area, with offices, shops, dressing-rooms, lounges, and rehearsal spaces. Carpentry shops are in a separate building across the street from the theatres. Administration is in another structure on the theatre plot. A Christian Science Church across the street has been acquired and is also used for rehearsal and studio performances.

Bowmer and Hay are by no means the only personnel who give impetus and continuity to the Festival. Jerry Turner, the present producing director, had staged plays at Ashland for nine seasons. To assume his present position, he gave up the chairmanship of the drama department of the University of California at Riverside. William Patton, who keeps the entire business operation under an amazingly calm control, has been general manager since 1953. Each season, four stage directors are responsible for the six productions.

Over the seasons, an impressive store of Elizabethan and other period costumes—as well as of furniture and properties—has been built up. The shops and storage areas are all well equipped places to work. A detailed and intelligent system of checking costumes and props in and out during productions has been set up. Thus any breaks, tears, soilages, or losses are immediately noted and taken care of.

In the 1973 season, the Festival's repute attracted so many theatre tourists that, of the 164 performance total, 108 were sold out. And the Bowmer theatre, with its 600 luxurious seats, averaged 91.8 percent of its capacity. In 1972, it was often only half or two-thirds full, and Bowmer, Turner, and Patton confidently expected it would take a decade for it to sell out regularly. In the meantime, it would provide an alternative for those improvident travellers who had not ordered tickets in advance. Now, in just four years, it, like the Elizabethan Theatre, has virtually reached its capacity. The summer 1973 total for both houses was 143,300 patrons.

The 1974 production season budget was $836,000. For this money, Ashland's Shakespeare program featured *Twelfth Night, Titus Andronicus, Hamlet,* and *Two Gentlemen of Verona.* The non-Bardic balance was provided by Saroyan's *Time of Your Life* and Beckett's *Waiting for Godot.* The other Ashland productions during the year—but not shown during the summer season—were Ibsen's *Hedda Gabler* and the musical, *A Funny Thing Happened on the Way to the Forum.* The 1975 season is composed of *Romeo and Juliet, All's Well That Ends Well,* and *Henry VI* in the Elizabethan Theatre, and *A Winter's Tale, Charley's Aunt,* and *Long Day's Journey into Night* in the Bowmer Theatre.

Because so many of the company have been students and teachers, the Festival's dates have formerly been dictated by semester endings and begin-

Troilus and Cressida staged at the Oregon Shakespearean Festival's indoor Angus Bowmer Theatre

nings. Recently, however, owing to a new Bowmer Theatre spring season, in March and April, appealing to students and adults during the traditional vacation period, and a single fall production, the Ashland operation is becoming increasingly a year-round affair. For the resident production staff, it has been that for some time. But now students who get scholarships for working in the ensemble often prefer to take a year off from their studies for this practical kind of training. Patton says, "We have about 45 people—actors and staff—in the fall, from October 1st to January 1st. Then the number jumps to about 85, preparing for the spring season. In the latter part of April, we bring in the final segment for the outdoor theatre, and the company goes up to about 165 members."

For the four spring shows, one or two of which survive into the summer, students are bused from the Canadian border in the North, from Idaho in the East and from the valleys and foothills of California in the South. The fall show is primarily for local spectators. Ancillary theatre, educational, and recreational activities have been devised to permit some expansion. They include such things as courses and seminars of the Institute of Renaissance Studies, founded by the late Margery Bailey of Stanford University; backstage tours; Wagon Theatre performances in Lithia Park, adjacent to the theatre-complex; Ashland Summer Concerts; Shakespeare-in-Action Talks; the Gresham Lecture Series; the Green Dancers and Tudor Fair, preceding each evening's performance; puppet and magic shows in the plaza outside the theatres; and the Peter Britt Gardens Music and Arts Festival in the historic—and restored—nearby mining town of Jacksonville.

An interesting dividend for Festival supporters is the possibility of joining an annual summer theatre tour of Great Britain, led by Professor and Mrs. Bowmer. Among the events of the 29-day jaunt are visits to the Edinburgh and Stratford Festivals.

The Taming of the Shrew *(facing page, top)*
Henry IV, Part II *(facing page, bottom left)*
Love's Labour's Lost *(facing page, bottom right, below)*
Titus Andronicus *(bottom)*

By 1958, Ashland had presented the complete canon. This record may soon be repeated. Ashland's professionalism has been attributed to three factors: talent, money, and audience. Its talent resources and its audiences have been noted. But its money reserves are another matter. Where Canada's Stratford Festival is munificently subsidised, Ashland's operation, according to William Patton, is almost entirely dependent on box-office sales. Ticket sales cover 95 percent of the operational costs. Some 5 per cent is raised by donations, and from profits from sales of souvenirs and refreshments in the theatres by civic groups. The Festival management is seeking to win more subsidy. In fact, they must, if they are to meet rising costs of materials, services, and wages without having to make the ticket prices also inflationary and forbidding.

The first giant step in this direction was an initial grant of $67,390 to further the Festival's Artists-in-the-School Program. Over half came from the National Endowment for the Arts, and the rest from the National Endowment for the Humanities, an interesting instance of cooperation. This grant had to be matched by the Festival, but only in terms of man-hours, skills, and equipment. In 1974, the project was in its third successful year. Unfunded but equally strongly encouraged are school and college junkets to Ashland for performances and instructor-conducted classes related to the plays. The Ashland staff, technicians, designers, and actors make themselves readily available to assist with such field-trip education.

What they have realized is that they are helping to create the audience of the future, without which there will be no more Ashland Festivals, perhaps no more living theatre.

San Diego National Shakespeare Festival

Old Globe Theatre/Cassius Carter
Centre Stage
Balboa Park
P. O. Box 2171
San Diego, California 92112
(714) 239–2255
administration: (714) 234–3601
Producing Director: Craig Noel

San Diego's Old Globe Theatre opened with its first Shakespearean productions in 1935. That was also Year One for the Oregon Shakespearean Festival. As things turned out, 1935 was not to be Year One for San Diego—nor had anything like an annual festival of the Bard's plays been envisioned. Thus, Ashland has clear title to the name of America's Oldest Shakespeare Festival. Like Avis, San Diego is Number 2.

1974 was San Diego's twenty-fifth anniversary as an annual event. The Festival, as in past years, justified the inclusion of "national" in its trade-name by recruiting its strong Equity company of over fifteen players from various parts of the nation. Its large group of young performers, sustained on acting grants, is drawn mainly from West Coast drama departments and theatre groups.

Its proximity to Hollywood permits the San Diego Festival to contract well known film and television actors for summer engagements in such roles as Iago or Richard III. Producing director Craig Noel, who has been with the Old Globe since its reorganization after World War II, has always tried to balance seasoned performers with enthusiastic newcomers. He provides a mixture of the known and the unknown which can produce potent on-stage chemistry, when the right director is compounding the elements.

In his directorial staff, Noel is also careful to maintain a balance of maturity and youth, conservatism and adventure. In recent seasons, such talented directors as Allen Fletcher, Eric Christmas, Ellis Rabb, Edward Payson Call, William Ball, Malcolm Black, and Milton Katselas have divided the tasks of staging the summer triple-bills.

Programming tends toward two comedies and a tragedy, with a history play now and then for variety. Craig Noel has been producing Shakespeare in San Diego long enough to know that comedy will entice more people to the Old Globe than tragedy.

This preference for comedy does not, of course, really reveal very much about the cultural tastes of San Diegans, since the Festival's fame now draws visitors from all over the United States and Canada, as well as from foreign countries. That is perhaps yet another reason why San Diego can safely call its Festival a national one.

When San Diego's Old Globe was first opened, it had a dubious boast: that it was "the only functioning replica of Shakespeare's original Globe Playhouse." Since so little is known with absolute certainty about the first Globe, whatever may be built can at present be no more than an evocation of an Elizabethan theatre. Today neither Noel nor his staff would insist on the Globe's authenticity, especially since the open-air pit for the groundlings has been roofed over for year-round theatre production.

The Old Globe came into being as an attraction of the California Pacific International Exposition in 1935. It was constructed in Balboa Park, now in the heart of modern San Diego. The Old Globe was crammed with Exposition visitors eager to enjoy the fifty-minute digest versions of Shakespeare's plays, offered by Thomas Wood Stevens and B. Iden Payne. Stevens and Payne had tried out this novelty with great success in 1933 at the Chicago "Century of Progress" Exhibition. San Diego's Old Globe was flanked by various mock-Tudor buildings, including a Falstaff Tavern, where hungry and thirsty spectators could refresh themselves in period style.

When the Old Globe and the outbuildings were sold to a wrecking company for $400 after two lively Exposition seasons, San Diegans became aroused. The theatre had won a place in their hearts. In a few weeks, $10,000 was raised for purchase and renovation, even though citizens were suffering from Depression privations. The city matched this with $10,000, and the WPA matched that with $20,000. The building, of course, was originally only intended

The Merchant of Venice

for a season or two of summer use. Its stucco and plywood had to be replaced with the greater permanence of concrete. Nonetheless, the Old Globe was now part of San Diego's tradition and it was not only to be rebuilt for survival but also for regular use. The community theatre, formerly housed in a remodeled barn, in 1937 moved into the Old Globe. During the war, all this activity came to a halt. The U.S. Navy, always a major operation in San Diego, took over the theatre and all the contents of Balboa Park except the Zoo. In 1947, Craig Noel was asked to bring the theatre back to life for the community. Then, in 1949, in cooperation with San Diego State College, the first summer Shakespeare Festival was produced. B. Iden Payne was recalled to the scene of his 1935–36 triumphs to direct *Twelfth Night*. For the next three years, two plays were presented each summer, but empty seats and deficits brought the work to a halt in 1953. Instead, Noel mounted *Mr. Roberts* for 69 performances, playing to 25,000 spectators. If that number seems impressive, it ought to be even more so, considering that the tiny Old Globe auditorium seats only 420 people.

In 1954, however, San Diegans showed they cared about their Shakespeare Festival and provided sufficient funds for the engagement of professional actors, free of college ties. Since that time, the Festival has systematically increased its Equity complement and enlarged its program of apprentices and scholarship-actors. In addition to its practice of engaging directors who have proven their worth, the Festival has also been careful to retain some of the best technical theatre talent available. Art Director Peggy Kellner, for example, is not only a gifted set and costume designer, but she is also Noel's strong right hand in planning and coordinating technical activities. Others whose work is nationally known are costume designer Douglas Russell, lighting designer John McLain, and composer Conrad Susa.

The Two Gentlemen of Verona

King Lear

The Old Globe's auditorium is small, and the stage area is similarly intimate. To provide good sight-lines and still evoke the feeling of Shakespeare's theatre, Peggy Kellner has devised a basic "Elizabethan" setting. With the aid of some step units, arches, and various flats, the basic areas can be quickly dressed up to represent the locales needed for the three plays always offered in the summer repertory. A limited overhead space permits some things to be flown as well. Backstage storage space is also limited, so design elements have to be kept simple. Stage crews are not large, owing to tight budgeting, so Ms. Kellner's artful minimality pays a variety of dividends.

What is especially helpful is the fact that the apron or thrust stage extends out 10' on each side from the proscenium opening. This picture-frame was once filled with the supposed inner-above and inner-below of the original Globe. By opening up a production through the frame—which is approximately 20' wide and 14' high—it is possible to have a much larger setting. Peggy Kellner uses this to great advantage during the Old Globe's regular season of modern plays, creating unbelievably spacious interiors in the seemingly miniscule area.

Costume, of course, has to do a lot in setting the time and tone of the production, given the necessary simplicity and minimality of setting and lighting. For a production of *Love's Labour's Lost,* Ms. Kellner's sets and costumes created the impression of a Fragonard painting come to life. Another production, memorable in every way, was Edward Payson Call's fine staging of *Twelfth Night* in 1967. Visually, intellectually, emotionally, it was so well integrated that it seemed near perfection.

Summer Shakespeare choices in 1974 were *Twelfth Night, Romeo and Juliet,* and *King Henry IV,* but what is worthy of special attention is the way in which the Festival has developed into a year-

The Two Gentlemen of Verona *(above)*
King Lear *(right)*

Peggy Kellner's costume sketches for King Lear

Edmund   Glouster   Edgar

round professional theatre operation. In effect, the Old Globe has become the San Diego regional theatre. Owing to the relatively few seats in the Old Globe and the steadily growing audiences, Craig Noel and his board were forced in 1968 to rebuild the Falstaff Tavern, turning it into the Cassius Carter Centre Stage. Named for a San Diegan who was an ardent theatre supporter, it is a square arena-stage complex. Opened in 1969, it provides a second house for the regular season and during the summer can serve as the scene of modern antidotes to too much Shakespeare.

In 1966, a $300,00 building project made possible a new rehearsal hall, offices, lounges, dressing-rooms, set and costume shops, and storage facilities. For most of its life, the San Diego Shakespeare venture has been supported by box-office receipts and local donations of money, goods, and services. San Diegans, Noel explains, tend to be conservative, and they look with distrust on government subsidies. Today, however, ticket sales and local benefactions are not enough. Production costs—materials, wages,

and similar items—are skyrocketing, but the Old Globe cannot expand. Ticket prices cannot be raised beyond a certain level, or the audience will be lost.

Fortunately, not only do San Diegans love visiting their Old Globe and its productions, but they also enjoy helping out on voluntary crews. Some of the younger and more energetic work backstage on sets and costumes. Others prefer the contact with the public that comes from working in the box-office, at the refreshment stands, and the concession stalls. And there is the fun of performing in the Festival Revels which precede each show. Musicians, tumblers, gypsy dancers, belly dancers, country dancers, fencers, jugglers, and even a fire-eater and a fortune-teller try to create the atmosphere of an Elizabethan fair.

The Shakespeare Society of America at The Globe Theatre

"One of these years while driving in the Santa Monica Mountains, you may come upon a full-sized replica of Shakespeare's Globe Theatre. Or the Tower of London, Hamlet's Castle, the Roman Colosseum, the pyramids of Egypt, or a columned Greek temple."

That is a quote from the *Los Angeles Times,* a newspaper which serves an area rich in fantasy and invention. The story the quote introduces describes the dreams of R. Thad Taylor, founder of the Shakespeare Society of America. What Taylor wants is 1,000 acres of a proposed 100,000 tract earmarked for a Santa Monica Mountains and Seashore National Urban Park.

On that acreage, he plans to build an International Cultural Center, taking his cue, he says, from Plato, St. Thomas More, Montaigne, Bacon, and, of course, Shakespeare. He envisions a kind of combination "cultural United Nations, the Olympics, and the World's Fair." This will feature reproductions of famous cultural landmarks, with live and filmed performances in appropriate national habitats.

Before this is dismissed as a pipe-dream, one shouldn't forget how many extant Shakespeare festivals would never have come into being, had it not been for the vision and determination of men and women even more fanatic than R. Thad Taylor.

Taylor's fanaticism—in the sense of an unremitting dedication to an idea—has already made its mark in Los Angeles. Proof may be found in the fact that he and his co-workers in the Shakespeare Society of America have succeeded in establishing a year-round program of Shakespeare-oriented production in their half-size replica of the Globe.

Currently, performances run from Thursdays through Sundays, with two performances on Sunday. In 1975, for instance, *The Tempest* ran from 14 February to 16 March. On Good Friday, the world premier of a new play by Ben Orkow took place.

1107 North Kings Road
Los Angeles, California 90069
(213) 650–0208/654–9100
Executive Producer: R. Thad Taylor

86

This drama, *The First Actress,* dealt with a lass who disguised herself to get on stage with Shakespeare. It ran for four weekends, followed by yet another world premier, this time *Shakespeare on Love.* The nominal author is a rather suspect "Christopher Bacon." Taylor proudly reveals that the true and "onlie" begetter of this entertainment—aside from the Bard himself—is none other than TV personality Steve Allen.

Hollywood and the surrounding stretches of Los Angeles have an overabundance of trained performers and theatre technicians, many of them with an over-abundance of free time. Taylor has been able to bring them, the Bard, and the Los Angeles public together for mutual benefits. Actor Avery Schreiber had his first contact with the classics when Taylor got him to appear in a Shakespeare Society show. One of the Society's first actors, Richard Ramos, scored a personal success as Bottom in a Joseph Papp production at Lincoln Center in 1975.

The Kings Road Globe seats only 99 spectators, so although it is using Equity card-holders, it qualifies as an Equity workshop. Which means that the actors donate their time, as does Taylor himself.

Taylor actually donates more than just his time. Asked how much subsidy he gets from the City and County of Los Angeles, he says, "None." From the State of California? "Nothing." From the National Endowment for the Arts? "Still nothing." The basic funding for this Shakespeare venture is Taylor's own money. In fact, he says, the largest donation the Society has ever received was $100. "There haven't been any outside grants," he says, a bit sadly. He's convinced that politics has something to do with it, but he is hopeful that the winds will change and blow more favorably upon his Bardic projects. Some funding comes from society membership: $15 for adults and $5 for students annually.

Shakespeare's dramas are the core of the work at Kings Road, but other classics and new plays are also programmed. Taylor directs when he has time, but more often he retains the services of directors like Jack Bender and Jack Manning.

The aims of the Society are stated officially thus: "Dedicated to Instruct [sic] and Advance the Works of William Shakespeare." Initially, Taylor decided to advance the works by producing them in a kind of open-air theatre formed by the facade of a Tudor mansion near the Sunset Strip. He saw in the lines of this structure some kinship to Shakespeare's home, New Place, in Stratford-upon-Avon. There, Taylor and his actors and his audiences found a home until 1972, when they were driven out by a developer. After a long search, Taylor found the present Kings Road location. On the outside, the building looks like nothing so much as a sheet-metal clad warehouse. Inside, however, is the intimate Taylor-designed version of the Globe.

And someday, if Taylor gets his 1,000 acres and his way, there will be another, larger Globe in the Santa Monica Mountains.

Elizabethan Court Masque, The Judgment of Paris

Stratford Festival of Canada

Canada's Stratford Festival is many things. One of them must surely be its character as a living, vital memorial to the dedication and talent of Sir Tyrone Guthrie who was so important to its founding and development. It is also, of course, a Shakespeare Festival, at present the only one in Canada. But its very success as a celebration of the Bard's genius has encouraged it to grow and change so significantly that the hallowed name of Shakespeare was quietly dropped from the title early in the 1970's.

Shakespeare associations are, however, so plentiful in Stratford, Ontario, that most Festival visitors scarcely notice that the Festival name has been changed. Not only is the town that is the Festival's home called Stratford, after its English namesake, but it also has an Avon River.

Tom Patterson, a Stratford-born journalist, thought his home town should have a Shakespeare festival, just as its English counterpart does. He won the attention of Dr. Guthrie, who investigated the site in Ontario in 1952. Dr. Guthrie became so interested that he agreed to be the first producer-director. An initial budget of $150,000 was proposed and accepted. Sir Alex Guinness and Irene Worth were the first stars.

Planning and fund-raising were undertaken by the Stratford Shakespearean Festival Foundation of Canada. In its 21st season in 1973, only three works by Shakespeare were offered in the repertory. For most of the American fests, three Shakespeare productions would be a quite respectable number, especially when they are *The Taming of the Shrew, Pericles,* and *Othello.* In Ontario though, they were only one-third of the productions offered. For retiring artistic director Jean Gascon's farewell Stratford season in 1974, *Love's Labour's Lost, Pericles,* and *King John* dominated the Festival Theatre's stage, representing the Shakespeare canon. They were balanced by Molière's *The Imaginary Invalid,* a lively Gascon-

P. O. Box 520
Stratford, Ontario, Canada N5A 6V2
(519) 273–1600
Artistic Director: Robin Phillips

Pericles *(left)*
Cymbeline *(below)*

Much Ado About Nothing *(above left)*
Othello *(above right)*
The Taming of the Shrew *(right)*

mounted production which had been acclaimed on the company's Australian tour. At the Avon Theatre, Offenbach's *La Vie Parisienne* was offered in an English version. The experimental Third Stage's most impressive premier was Sharon Pollock's drama of Sitting Bull's ordeal in Canada, *Walsh.* Also shown were a children's show, *Ready Steady Go,* by Sandra Jones, and two contemporary opera productions, Charles Wilson's *The Summoning of Everyman,* and Gian-Carlo Menotti's *The Medium,* starring Canadian contralto Maureen Forrester. In addition, Stratford also provided concerts, master classes, and an international film festival. As Gascon's successor, Robin Phillips has promised to explore the new directions which have been opened up and to do everything possible to help develop Canadian talents.

Shakespeare's plays and other classics which require large-scale production are staged in the Festival Theatre. In the intimate Avon Theatre, handsomely remodelled from its earlier architectural identity, both smaller plays and operas have been given.

In addition to the seven productions of the company, which is now called the Stratford National Theatre of Canada, other Canadian troupes are scheduled. In 1971, for instance, the Montreal Marionettes and the Canadian Mime Theatre were on hand. Festival visitors, whether tourist or student, are also offered various Shakespeare-related treats such as special art exhibits, collections of props and costumes from previous seasons, and even a garden planted with flora mentioned in the Bard's dramas. Students can delve deeper with Drama Workshops and Shakespeare Seminars. Tourists can while away

The Merchant of Venice

Alan Barlow costume designs for Much Ado About Nothing *(this page right and far right)*, Desmond Heeley's designs for Richard III *(facing page, left and right)*, and Tanya Moiseiwitsch's design for King John *(facing page, center)*

an hour rowing on the Avon. Or they can play Gulliver in a Lilliputian recreation of historic buildings in the original Stratford. This curiosity is called Shakespeareland, and it is convenient to the *As You Like It* Motel. As in the parent Stratford, the Shakespeare whimsey can seem excessive now and then. Many Festival visitors enjoy staying in private homes and getting to know their Canadian neighbors better. The impact of the Festival on Stratford, in terms of food, lodging, services, and souvenir sales, has been tremendous. The Ontario Department of Tourism early in the 1970's indicated that over $8,000,000— exclusive of theatre admissions— was being spent in Stratford every summer. Currently, box-office grosses for combined drama and music offerings are approaching $2,000,000 per season.

This is an amazing record, considering that Stratford was a sleepy little agricultural town of some 20,000 inhabitants in 1953. It is, of course, partly a testimony to Shakespeare's drawing power. There is magic in the Bard's name. But it is also a testimony to the belief of the Canadian people in the importance of performing arts in the nation's cultural life.

Despite the impressive box-office grosses, this Festival, like almost all the others, is a money-losing operation. Without its hefty subsidies from the Canada Council, the Province of Ontario Council for the Arts, and the Ontario Department of Education, Stratford's fine fest would not exist, or certainly not at its present level of activity and excellence. Government subsidy provides 18–20 percent of the annual budget, says recently retired director Jean Gascon. In 1966, the Board of Governors began annual campaigns for production and improvement funding. That year $100,000 was donated from the business and private sectors. In 1971, $194,292 was received, but 1973's target was $300,000. In 1970, Ontario retired 54 percent of previous production deficits. By 1975, the Canada Council will have retired the rest, in five annual installments. After this date, deficits will not be allowed to accumulate.

Such handsome financial support—and the moral support that goes with it—has done much to reinforce the high standards of production and performance which distinguish what has rightly become a National Theatre. But the Stratford Festival ensemble was not created overnight, nor was money itself enough to lure Dr. Guthrie and such successors as Michael Langham and Jean Gascon to shape the enterprise with such skill and care. At first, English

stars, English directors, and English designers left their imprint on the Festival. Very soon, however, with strong encouragement from their English colleagues, Canadian artists were making their names known, not only in Stratford but also on Broadway and in London. Such names as Christopher Plummer, Douglas Campbell, Martha Henry, Douglas Rain, Frances Hyland, William Hutt, and Donald Davis.

Although Dr. Guthrie, Langham, Douglas Seale, Peter Hall, and Peter Coe gave the Festival a strong spine of British stage direction, Canada was producing its own: men like the able French Canadian actor-director, Jean Gascon; George McGowan, and John Hirsch. In the late 1960's, the company they had helped develop was regarded by many experts as the finest ensemble in North America, virtually on a par with Great Britain's Royal Shakespeare Company or its National Theatre. Under Gascon's artistic direction, the challenge did not slacken, the programming, if anything, became even more adventurous, especially in offering a showcase for new Canadian writing and composing talents. At times, however, the company did not seem quite as strong as it had been, but such things can change from season to season. In 1972, for instance, William Hutt's *King Lear* was less rewarding than had been expected, but the same ensemble's *She Stoops To Conquer,* featuring the gifted comedienne Carole Shelley, was a superb, almost definitive production.

Counting rehearsals and school performances at the beginning and end of the season, which now extends over twenty-three weeks, this Equity troupe has plenty of experience with classic and contemporary works, like its British twin, the Royal Shakespeare Company. With Canadian tours, American engagements, and foreign visits, production at Stratford is becoming a year-round business. Actors are engaged for nearly eleven months out of twelve. Its regular staff numbers over seventy, and some 650 people are on its payroll at the height of the summer season. These include not only directors, designers, actors, musicians, and technical staff, but also secretaries, cooks, gardeners, and "go-fors" to help with the myriad details involved in running what has become an international festival. Its visitors come largely from Canada and the United States, but over fifty other lands have been included in its audiences, from Bermuda to Uganda.

The permanent theatre, designed by Robert Fairfield, and incorporating stage-structure ideas from Dr. Guthrie and designer Tanya Moiseiwitsch's 1953 tent-stage, won the Massey Gold Medal for Architecture in 1958. The stage is actually a skillful combination of platforms, stairs, levels, and portals which suggest the areas of an Elizabethan stage without any period detail or decor. It has a portico jutting out onto its thrust stage area. This upper level is supported on five pillars, reduced from an original nine. In addition to the balcony effect, there are trapdoors, six acting levels, and nine major entrances—some onstage and some from vomitoria in the semi-circular seating. In 1961, Ms. Moiseiwitsch and Brian Jackson made changes in the stage, dictated by experiences of the previous three seasons and with the intent of accentuating the intimate actor-audience relationship. They certainly succeeded.

Actually, no spectator is more than 65 feet from the stage. The steeply tiered seating arcs the stage on three sides with a 220° sweep. It seats 2,258 people—400 in the orchestra, 858 in the balcony—and is often sold out, even though, with the Avon and the Third Stage, over three hundred performances are played each season. The auditorium is comfortable but neutral, to focus attention on the stage. It, in turn, is also a neutral wood grain, focussing attention on the costumed actors, on their thoughts, their passions, and their movements. As in most arena or "Globe" reproductions, almost no scenery is needed or desired. Costumes, furniture, banners, and other props are all that are needed to create Shakespeare's worlds, whether they be ancient Rome, feudal Britain, or Renaissance Italy.

A $400,000 system maintains an even 72° temperature in the theatre. It is cool in summer, warm in winter. In 1972, a new stage-lighting and sound system was installed over the auditorium in a series of skillfully designed coves. This greatly increased flexibility in light and sound, as well as the amount

Pericles (top)
Love's Labour's Lost (above)

of instrumentation. There are twenty-four speakers with a twenty-four channel potential for mixing music and sound-effects with varying volumes where and as desired. A taped animal noise, for example, can seem to run around the auditorium, rising and falling at will. Control booths are behind the balcony, facing the stage. An orchestra loft is above and behind the stage, the music being deflected into the auditorium by a special acoustic ceiling.

The backstage area is one of the largest in any North American theatre. Administrative offices and technical shops, as well as dressing-rooms, cafeteria, lounges, and storage spaces are located on six levels. All props and costumes are constructed on the premises. Out front or backstage, there is nothing tentative, unprofessional, or make-shift about Canada's Stratford Festival.

For the 1975 season, England's Robin Phillips succeeds Jean Gascon. Phillips has attracted the attention of drama critics for his stagings at England's Chichester Festival, which has a stage inspired by and similar to that of Ontario's Stratford. Phillips has also been praised for his work in forming the Company Theatre, with leading British stars who performed the classics for short runs and little pay at the Greenwich Theatre, far from London's theatre center, the West End. That kind of operation contrasts quite strongly with the Stratford enterprise, which is budgeted at over $3,000,000 annually.

Shakespeare's name will always receive its due at Stratford. As Jean Gascon has said, "We believe we should go on producing Shakespeare because he is the Grandfather—or the God—of this place. It brings in the bread-and-butter. Shakespeare is probably the most extraordinary dramatist who ever existed!"

The Stratford Festival Theatre exterior and modern thrust stage interior *(below and bottom)*

Shakespeare in the Summer

Alabama Shakespeare Festival

P.O. Box 141
Anniston, Alabama 36201
(205) 237–2332
June–August
Artistic Director: Martin Platt

Until the opening of the Alabama Shakespeare Festival in Anniston in 1972, the only summer entertainment in the area was the Talladega 500 stock car race at a nearby speedway. It is highly doubtful that Shakespeare will ever beat the stock cars in popular entertainment polls, but festival artistic director Martin Platt and his band of enthusiastic actors, designers, and apprentices are doing their best to put Shakespeare on the map in the Southeast.

Walking through the quiet, tree-lined streets of Anniston, the obvious question is: why did this small Southern town get into the Shakespeare business? The festival is the brain child of Martin Platt, a Carnegie-Mellon University graduate who was looking for something to do with his summers. He was already directing the local Little Theatre in Anniston during the winter. Local notables who supported Little Theatre activities were eager to expand into summer Shakespeare support. Ultimately, of course, these businessmen all knew that the town would benefit from the success of the festival.

Geographically, Anniston is a likely spot for a Shakespeare Festival. It is the only resident one in the Southeastern United States. Other than annual festivities surrounding the Globe Theatre reconstruction at Columbus College in Georgia, the closest festival is the Globe of the Great Southwest in Odessa, Texas. In addition, Anniston is on the main highway between Birmingham and Atlanta. Martin Platt notes that during their second season, they could only count on 300–400 local residents as regular festival playgoers, so to succeed they had to try drawing regularly on patrons from Birmingham, Atlanta, and ultimately from the whole Southeast.

Already, it appears that their predictions are coming true. Second season attendance was up over the first season. By the third summer, the festival even found itself playing to sold out houses. The festival is being reviewed in local papers, as well as in Birmingham and Atlanta, and being mentioned in national press. Theatre buffs have driven up from New Orleans to see productions, and reviews of the Alabama plays have appeared in Eastern Texas newspapers. With the proper promotion and publicity, they can see the festival becoming at least a one-night draw for tourists in the area—and, perhaps even the purpose of the trip, as the Oregon Shakespearean Festival is for many of its visitors.

Anniston, Alabama's first season in 1972, which was launched on a loan of $500, ran 31 performances. Eventually they did get a small grant from the Alabama Arts Council. That first season they staged three Shakespeare plays, *Comedy of Errors*, *Two Gentlemen of Verona* (a Victorian Gilbert and Sullivan version), and a black-and-white design *Hamlet*. In addition they also put on Ibsen's *Hedda Gabler*. The festival was housed in the Little Theatre's space, a former high school auditorium, which featured a stage that doubled as a basketball court, no flying facilities, terrible acoustics, 22 lighting instruments, and worst of all, no air conditioning. In spite of all the negative factors, by the end of their first season, audience response indicated that the Anniston area was ready for Shakespeare.

When it became clear that the Alabama Shakespeare Festival was more than a one-summer fling interested local businessmen lent a hand. The festival became a non-profit corporation, complete with a wisely-selected Board of Directors which includes bankers and public relations people, headed by none other than Mrs. George Wallace. Arrangements were made to rent the only other auditorium in town—a modern, air-conditioned space in the new high school building. Financial support was forthcoming from a number of sources: the Alabama State Arts Council, an anonymous donor, the Chamber of Commerce, the local TV and newspapers, program advertising, and the city. All told they raised about

The Taming of the Shrew

$7,500 for the 1973 season. Tickets were priced at $3, and $2 for students. The gate made up all but a few thousand dollars of their $26,000 budget.

The second summer season in 1973 ran for 4½ weeks, and featured three Shakespeare plays, plus Molière's *Tartuffe*. Artistic Director Platt notes that he thinks it is more fun for both the actors and the audience when the majority of plays selected for the season are comedies. Their *Macbeth* was a straight medieval Scotland—cold, and barren with lots of dark tartans. Molière's *Tartuffe* was also true to its period. *Much Ado About Nothing* was charmingly staged as an Antebellum South battle between Beatrice and Benedict. *As You Like It* was transformed into a rock musical using Shakespeare songs, setting some verse to music and including new works.

The Festival's new high school auditorium theatre was not without its complications. Audience comfort was up 100 percent over the 1972 summer. But difficulties stemmed from the strange quirks in the design of the theatre. Local people claim they never meant to have anything but lectures and beauty pageants in the space. It is basically a proscenium house, with seating arranged in a horseshoe-shape around a floor-level, 44' by 33' open thrust tongue. For the 1973 season it was only natural when staging Shakespeare to curtain off the proscenium and use the thrust floor. Without central or stage right vomitories, the actors spent a lot of time sneaking around the audience to make various entrances. For the 1974 summer season of *Midsummer Night's Dream, Romeo and Juliet, Taming of the Shrew,* and Molière's *School for Wives*, a raked thrust stage was designed and constructed to stand in the space—alleviating design and staging problems inherent in the auditorium.

The theatre has tried several different ways of solving their design requirements. For the 1973 season, a series of basic units was rearranged to make

As You Like It

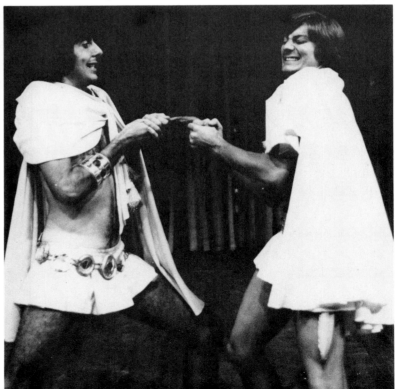

Romeo and Juliet *(above)*
As You Like It *(right top)*
A Midsummer Night's Dream *(right)*

up the setting for all of the season's plays. In that same year, Mary White was the resident costumer; and although overworked and hampered by a lack of funding and an apprentice costume crew, she managed to construct garments for both *Macbeth* and *As You Like It.* The other two shows were rented from Eaves in New York or the nearby Atlanta Costume Company.

For the 1974 summer, director Platt found design talent for the Festival at the University of Alabama. Faculty member Alan Armstrong designed costumes for three shows which were also constructed in the University's shops. He has gone on to the University of California at Santa Barbara, but will return to design for the 1975 season. The 1974 budget was stretched by renting one show—*Romeo and Juliet*— from the Theatre Development Fund-administered Costume Collection. John Ross, another University of Alabama faculty member, created a different scenic solution for each production.

In the first three summers of its existence, the Alabama Shakespeare Festival underwent considerable change and growth. The shoestring operation of the first year became a modestly produced festival the second year—one with difficulties to overcome but considerable potential. The designers and the director were quite visibly not comfortable on the stage they had to work with. The new thrust stage should result in productions that are both better staged and better designed. Further with a modest $26,000 budget, Platt did not have enough funds to lure professional and polished acting talent to what many might think of as the cultural wasteland of Alabama. Nor was the Festival so well-established that actors and designers would work just for the credit.

By the third summer design difficulties were solved by the new stage and a close association with designers on the staff of the University of Alabama. Festival attendance was up, as was the budget. The

$40,000 budget enabled the Festival to hire more auxiliary staff, expand the apprentice program and produce more fully-realized programs.

For the 1975 season of *The Tempest, Richard II, Twelfth Night* and Feydeau's *Fittings for Ladies,* director Martin Platt projects a $60,000 budget. The Alabama Shakespeare Festival seems slated for many successful seasons to come. The community is excited and supportive, their regional press is good. There are all the indications that the festival is filling a need in the area and will continue to grow. The nearby *Birmingham News* echoes local enthusiasm for the festival: "The overall effect of what we see virtually rivals the three Stratfords, and serves to establish Anniston as the next likely site for a permanent Festival in North America."

The Taming of the Shrew *(left and far left)*

Champlain Shakespeare Festival

At the University of Vermont in Burlington, two kinds of theatre work come together each summer to make possible an interesting balance of professional and student cooperation. The focus of this activity is the university's Champlain Shakespeare Festival, named for neighboring Lake Champlain. Edward Feidner, who is Festival Producer, a play director, and head of the drama program, makes it clear that a theatre major at Vermont is an intensive experience in the liberal arts, not a professional training course.

Nonetheless, during the Festival, drama students have the opportunity to work alongside youthful professionals, which gives them a taste of the skills and discipline necessary to perform a rotating repertory of three Shakespeare plays each summer season. As Feidner says, "For those students who feel this is possibly their life's work, we provide an entrée to the theatre through the Festival, which is concerned with the young professional."

Recent seasons have offered such acting talents as Jason Miller, author of *That Championship Season*; Carole Demas, praised for her work on Broadway in *Grease,* and Randy Kim, frequently featured in New York productions. That does not mean that the atmosphere of this Festival is one of glitter and startime. Not at all. In fact, Feidner insists, "I'm not really interested in national publicity." The business of his department is liberal education. The business of the Champlain Festival is to provide the best possible Shakespearean stagings, given the time, budget, playing space, and talent available.

The Festival was the first fully professional theatre in Vermont. There is a basic core of about 12 Equity actors. Some are auditioned in New York. Some return from a previous season. Some have been seen elsewhere, in performance and are invited to Burlington. Wherever they have been discovered, they find in this Festival an operation which is de-

Royall Tyler Theatre/Univ. of Vermont
Burlington, Vermont 05401
(802) 656-2094
July–September
Producing Director: Edward J. Feidner

Richard III *(left)*
Cymbeline *(below)*
The Merry Wives of Windsor *(bottom)*

signed to help them get more experience. But, as Feidner points out, "It's a rare actor I will invite back for a third season . . . I don't think this should become a home or a womb to return to." The salaries are minimal, he notes, and if after three to six years, an actor still cannot make a living wage, perhaps he should think about some other career.

In performance, differences in the talent and training levels of the professionals sometimes intrude, but there is a real sense of enthusiasm and vitality in the ensemble which more than makes up for that. After all, producing Shakespeare is still a learning experience for both the pros and the students.

Both groups are certainly doing something right, for seats were often sold out in the old intimate Arena Theatre, and this is still true in the new Royall Tyler Theatre. Festival visitors come from Canada as well as forty-eight of the states. The repertory they see is customarily composed of a tragedy, a chronicle play, and a comedy by Shakespeare. In 1972, *Titus Andronicus* was boldly presented, even though most producing organizations are afraid to tackle it. *Troilus and Cressida* and Marlowe's difficult *Edward II* have also been staged, demonstrating the courage of this enterprising Festival. For the 1974 Shakespeare season, Feidner programmed a challenging bill: *Cymbeline, Hamlet,* and *The Tempest.* The directors, respectively, were Nancy Haynes, Michael Diamond, and Feidner.

The Festival came into being in 1959, as part of the 350th anniversary celebration of the discovery of Lake Champlain. It was founded by Greg Falls, who helped it win an award from the New England Theatre Conference that first season. In 1958, Feidner had joined the drama staff as a stage and technical director.

In March 1974, the Royall Tyler Theatre became the Festival's new home. Like the old Arena, however, the Tyler was built into a pre-existing struc-

The Tempest *(above)*
As You Like It *(right top)*
Hamlet *(right)*

106   Champlain Shakespeare Festival

ture. This time it was the old gym-auditorium, a handsome brick and masonry building dating from 1901.

Taking its name from Royall Tyler, author of America's first successful comedy, the new house is a fitting locale for the Bard's comedies. (Boston-born, Tyler settled in Vermont where the natives adopted him as one of their own.) The auditorium seats 350 on three sides of a flexible thrust stage. Seats on the right and left sides are removable chairs; in front of the stage, the seating is fixed. The stage is 33' by 30' with offstage space measuring 26' by 98'.

The Festival ambience has always been very pleasant, even before the new theatre did away with the old Arena's handicaps. Burlington itself is an impressive New England center, with a number of handsome old churches and beautiful Victorian mansions. It would be well worth a visit, were the Festival not already a magnet for tourists.

As at several other Shakespearean fests, there are pre-performance entertainments. Strolling minstrels enliven the summer evenings. In the 1970's, the theatre apprentices were taught English country dances which they now demonstrate on the campus greensward. Booths with food, drink, and crafts are also regular features.

In keeping with the departmental emphasis on educational values, the Festival's run was extended into September in 1973. This late closing, unusual for most of the festivals, is designed to give returning University of Vermont students an opportunity to see the productions.

This obviously benefits the students in general, as well as being of special value to English and drama majors. Of more immediate concern to drama students, however, are such Festival facts as Feidner's recruitment of campus non-professional actors, and the Repertory Theatre Operation Course.

This course carries up to nine units of university credit. It is designed to give students practical experience in professional theatre operation. From one point of view, it provides the Festival with a fee-paying, hard-working corps to handle much of the technical detail and theatre routine involved in building and caring for sets, costumes, and props and similar tasks. Apprentices also pay for their own room and board. From another viewpoint, however, it gives students not only the experience of learning-by-doing, but it also introduces them to the discipline and sense of responsibility so necessary to an effective theatre operation. In addition, Festival directors, actors, designers, and special instructors from the professional theatre or other universities guide student work and conduct discussion sessions in their respective areas.

Working with the acting company, apprentices, and volunteers are Feidner and a Festival staff. He often directs two of the three plays, inviting a guest director such as Ada Brown Mather, formerly of the Royal Academy of Dramatic Art, to direct the third.

In 1965, an Institute on Elizabethan Arts and Literature was established, with the aid of government funds. Well known scholars were invited to share their knowledge of Shakespeare's plays and his period with students. The five-week program included the last two weeks of rehearsals and the first three weeks of performances, to give students a chance to study their subject both in depth and in production. With fiscal belt-tightening in 1969, it was necessary to shelve the Institute temporarily, but Feidner hopes to find funds to revive it.

Over half the operation costs of the Champlain Festival come from the university as a direct subsidy. The remainder comes from box-office sales. Actually the budget is modest, made possible by thrift and the various economies of arena staging. Feidner is not eager for outside subsidies anyway. He believes the university should be committed to the living theatre.

Colorado Shakespeare Festival

*University of Colorado,
Boulder, Colorado 80302
(303) 443–2211*

*July–August
Executive Director: Albert H. Nadeau*

A mile high in the Rockies, and surrounded by still higher mountains, sits the town of Boulder. It is not far from Denver, and on the way to the breath-taking views, 12,000 foot passes, and tundra grasses in Rocky Mountain National Park. Everything in and around Boulder seems dominated by those mountains. Town ordinances keep the heights of buildings low—so not to obstruct the view. On afternoons when the Colorado Shakespeare Festival is in progress at the University, everyone looks to the mountains—watching for storm clouds which might cancel the outdoor performances. Sitting in the Mary Rippon Theatre, after the evening's Shakespeare entertainment has begun, the temperature quickly drops as it does only in deserts and mountains. Overhead the stars, on a cloudless night, are the kind that cowboys wrote songs about.

Since 1958, the Colorado Shakespeare Festival has been staged in this rather peaceful town, as part of the University of Colorado's Creative Arts Program. In 1973, *Twelfth Night, Hamlet,* and *Pericles* ran in repertory for 17 days from late July through August. In 1974, with a program of *Macbeth, Timon of Athens,* and *Midsummer Night's Dream,* the festival ran for 20 performances. The Festival has become a pleasantly anticipated event and citizens from Denver and surrounding towns come back year after year. In fact, the Festival has become so integrated into the summer life of the area that the Iliff School of Theology has featured a summer course which includes attendance at the Festival, and then discussions of the "religious values of the Bard's plays."

The Colorado Festival has earned this kind of loyalty. The work they do is good. It may not always be exciting—sometimes it is far from the mark, other times, it is right on. This is basically university theatre; and while university theatre can be as good as, or better than, the best professional theatre—you cannot always count on it.

108

Hamlet *(top)*
Macbeth *(above)*
Pericles *(right top)*
The Winter's Tale *(right)*

Macbeth *(above)*
Twelfth Night *(right)*

Albert Nadeau, the University's Theatre and Dance Department chairman, under whose auspices the Festival is carried out, points out that the Festival is largely self-supporting, but a subsidy from the University's Creative Arts Program enables them to invite guest directors, hire a technical staff, and award actor scholarships. In 1973, two directors, Daniel S. P. Yang and James Sandoe, were University faculty members, and the third, Gordon Wickstrom, came from Franklin and Marshall College in Pennsylvania. In 1974, the Festival directors included Martin Cobin, former Chairman of the Department of Communication and Theatre and frequent Festival director; Robert Baruch, former University of Colorado student and now a faculty member of the University of Wisconsin at Stevens Point; and Ricky Weiser, who has served the Festival in numerous and varied capacities since its first season.

The 1973 Festival acting company numbered about 37, and in 1974 the company grew to 44, which included faculty members from other universities, recruits from national touring theatre companies, a number of Boulder residents, plus other University students. In 1974, the administrative, design, and production staff numbered 12, while the backup crew of costume, scenic and technical assistants numbered 22. Included in these numbers were 20 scholarship actors who were paid between $400–$600 each; 6 administrative assistants ($350–$1000), 8 technical assistants ($250–$1,200), and 14 costume assistants ($400–$800).

In 1973, the Festival experimented with a national design competition, the results of which determined the designers and the design of the season's first production, *Twelfth Night*. Gail Argetsinger created a Son-of-Zorro, Spanish Flamenco costume look to complement Charles Bjorklund's lacy boxwood hedges and bushes.

Scene designer/technical director Dan Dryden and

Robert Morgan's costume sketches for Antony and Cleopatra, Menas and Octavius *(left and below)*, and for The Winter's Tale, a woman *(bottom)*

costumer Deborah Dryden tried to find a solution to the Mary Rippon Theatre's outdoor scale problem in their production of *Hamlet*. Ten 12–18' screens confined the available staging area to a small portion of the whole. Heavily scaled and decorated costumes further concentrated the visual weight in one area of the stage. It was workable despite local objections that they were tampering with the theatre.

For the 1973 season's final production *Pericles*, Thomas Schmunk designed a 120-costume, Byzantine "special" with little more scenery than a few benches and tables. During the six seasons from 1968–1973, while Schmunk (the University's resident costumer) also served as the Festival costume designer and artistic director, the Colorado Festival became famous for the high quality of its costuming.

Until the 1974 season, with the exception of occasional shows like the 1972 *Volpone* or the 1973 *Hamlet*, settings have never really been an important part of a show's design concept. The costumes set the visual tone while the scenic solutions fell into the bench-and-banner school of Shakespearean set design. And with good reason. The Colorado Festival is blessed with what is probably the most difficult of all the festival stages. The 1973 production staff fondly referred to it as the Mary-Rippon-Memorial-NFL-Outdoor-Theatre. The stage is a mammoth 72' by 64' covered with astroturf. Watching a production on that stage was closely akin to sitting at the 50-yard line or, even worse, watching a tennis match.

Built in the late 1930's, the Mary Rippon Theatre is dropped into a rectangle formed by four University buildings. An arc of stone benches provides seating for 1000. Fifteen foot towers on stage left and right are used for lighting positions. The Renaissance/Romanesque facade of the University Museum forms the back wall of the stage. Not a bad place to begin royal processions and a wonderful spot to stage huge battles—both of which the Festival has tried. But it would take a cast of cheap extras, rivaling the size of D. W. Griffith's *Intolerance* crew, to make the stage seem well used. It was not an easy space to work in and a continual battle raged over whether to leave the theatre alone as the 1973 *Pericles* did or whether to try to make the space work more effectively as the *Hamlet* did.

By the 1974 season the Colorado Festival had opted for an experimental scenic unit which is set into the Mary Rippon theater so that the acting area is confined to the theatre's flagstone apron, and the stage's wooden platforms circled by panels of vertical and horizontal wooden slats. The Rippon's side stages are still used for some scenes. University theatre designer Joseph Zender commented, "The intent is to rely on this basic structure for all shows in the Festival. The productions will be individualized 'on top' of this structure, with set-props, hangings and several alteration possibilities within the structure. With any luck we may eliminate the 60 ' crosses and the feeling that nature really is winning after all."

During the last several seasons, the Festival has been slowly undergoing changes in direction and leadership—at least in terms of administration and design, if not in stage direction. Richard Knaub, who had been producing director since 1966, resigned in 1971. Edgar Reynolds took on the job for the 1972 Festival. For 1973 and 1974, department head Albert Nadeau served as Festival executive director. With the 1973 Festival artistic director/costumer Thomas Schmunk resigned. His successor on the University faculty, Marianne Custer, designed one 1974 show and moved onto another position. Nancy Poulos and David Busse designed costumes for the 1974 season's other two shows. Instead of bringing scenic designers in from other parts of the country as they did in 1973, in 1974 the University's resident scene designer, Joseph Zender, served as Festival technical director and scenic designer. Two of the shows were designed by Tom Miller who is working on his Ph.D. at the University. With these frequent changes in the administrative and design goals of the Festival, it seems likely that the Colorado Festival has survived the last several seasons by virtue of academic perpetual motion rather than a conscious artistic decision and direction.

By the same token, the ups and downs of management seem to have had a beneficial effect on the potential audiences. In 1974, the Festival income was $51,433 of which $43,355 came from ticket sales, while their expenses were $51,827. For 17 performances in 1971, the audience was 13,159; for 16 performances in 1972 the total was down to 8,775; for 1973's 17 performances, 16,931 attended; and in 1974, the Colorado Festival played 20 performances for 18,693.

And for the future, in 1975 the Festival will complete the canon (production of all 37 of Shakespeare's plays) with the staging of *Cymbeline* directed by Festival founder Jack Crouch.

Great Lakes Shakespeare Festival

Lakewood Civic Auditorium
14100 Franklin Blvd. at Bunts Road
Lakewood, Ohio 44107
(216) 228–1225
July–September
Producing Director: Lawrence Carra

Inaugurated in 1962, the Great Lakes Shakespeare Festival is—to be quite precise—associated with only one of the Great Lakes, Lake Erie. Lakewood, an attractive western suburb of Cleveland, borders on Erie's impressive expanse of water. The Civic Auditorium, a large, conventional proscenium arch theatre, is near the lake. It is actually part of a large public high school, but was designed to serve both educational and community recreational needs.

In order to provide adult programs, the Cleveland Symphony and a ballet company were scheduled for winter engagements, but the huge house was still empty in summer. The Antioch College Shakespeare production venture, in Yellow Springs, Ohio, was still in operation in 1962, and it was invited to bring its entire repertory to Lakewood. This was done for four years, ending with the 1965 season when financial problems terminated its activities.

Lawrence Carra became the Festival's producer-director in 1966. Carra, as a theatre professor at Carnegie-Mellon University in Pittsburgh, Pennsylvania, had a pool of well trained students from which he could readily draw. And, since its drama graduates often go on to professional careers, Carra could easily make his company a completely Equity operation. That doesn't mean that the Festival is a closed-shop; Carra auditions to obtain the best performers he can for the season and salaries he has to offer—it is a LORT company, B Scale—regardless of where they were trained. Whether the immediate needs in the late 1960's were artistic or technical, Carra knew where he could turn for aid in an emergency. Now his actors get Equity scale or better. His technical apprentices get room-and-board and experience. "Enough to satisfy their needs," he says.

The Festival is not a Carnegie-Mellon activity. It is proudly and distinctively Lakewood's own gift to Cleveland citizens and Shakespeare pilgrims. As such, it is subsidised and supported in other ways by a long roster of Benefactors, Sponsors, Patrons, and Sustaining Members. Although many of the donors' names are preceded by the title "Dr.," there are also a number of foundations, businesses, and corporations represented, giving a broad base of support. A particularly interesting subsidy, from the Martha Holden Jennings Foundation and the Ohio Arts Council, enables student groups to see Festival productions in September for little or nothing.

The fact that the Great Lakes Shakespeare Festival often finishes its season in the black does not mean that it is a profit-making operation or that subsidies are unnecessary. Were it not for the generous community funding, there would be no end-of-season black to be in. That small margin of seeming profit is, of course, plowed back into the following year's Festival. And that profit is, like the subsidy which makes it possible, also owing to the community's support. Carra says that approximately 30 percent of the Festival costs are guaranteed by various subsidies and donations.

A specific and noteworthy example of local support is cited by Fred Youens, the Festival's lighting designer and technical director: Discussing the small production budget—often as little as $4,000 to set, costume, and light five different plays in repertory—Youens says, "All the materials are purchased locally. One thing we like to maintain is a good community relationship, which we do with businesses. They give us discounts. They really support us in terms of supplies and services."

The Great Lakes season runs some thirteen to fourteen weeks. Rehearsals begin about three weeks before the first opening night, making an actor or technician's total summer commitment nearly four months long. For professionals, this is a fine guarantee of employment. For apprentices, it provides a good taste of professional discipline as well as a variety of theatre experiences.

The repertory usually includes three Shakespeare plays: a comedy, a chronicle, and a tragedy. Two other plays, ancient or modern classics, round out the bill. During the summer of 1974, *King Lear* and *The Comedy of Errors* were both directed by Carra. Henry Hewes, drama critic for *Saturday Review* staged *Measure for Measure.* Carra also mounted productions of Synge's *Playboy of the Western World,* and Daly's American melodrama, *Under the Gaslight.* For the 1975 season the Great Lakes Shakespeare, which also bills itself as "Northern Ohio's summer professional repertory theatre," is expanding its season to run from July 3 through September, in order to accommodate a week of touring to universities in the area. The season includes *As You Like It, Our Town, Winter's Tale,* and a revised version of *The Frogs* with Stephen Sondheim music (first performed at Yale Repertory during 1974), plus Molière's *The Miser,* which will be staged by Jean Gascon, former artistic director of The Stratford Festival in Ontario. Not only do all five productions have to share that modest production budget—which fortunately doesn't include labor costs—but each one has a rehearsal period of only two to three weeks. Often it is closer to two than to three. That time limit applies to the building of settings and creation of complete costumes as well, but it can be cut to ten days. By the opening week, Carra's ensemble has two productions playing in alternating repertory, with two in rehearsal. By season's close, the company is capable of playing all five in rotation, surely something of a professional achievement.

It is true that such short rehearsal and construction periods have long been the custom in summer stock operations, so that is not in itself so remarkable. What is worthy of note is that the Great Lakes productions are creditable, professional work, which is not often the case in summer stock.

Hamlet Collage by Charles Marowitz *(above)*
Richard III (facing page, top)
Twelfth Night *(facing page, bottom)*

William French costume designs for A Midsummer Night's Dream: Titania *(top)*, Hippolyta *(above)*, Puck and Theseus *(facing page, top and bottom)*

Just because Shakespeare and other classic playwrights are being produced is no reason to perform them with academic pedantry or to mount them in a safely conventional manner. Nor do Carra and his guest directors make either of those usually boring mistakes. Without doing harm to the fabric of the dramas, Great Lakes directors try to find new ways of looking at the old favorites. Charles Marowitz's unusual *Hamlet Collage* has been presented, staged by Marowitz who came from London just for the Festival engagement. If it did more to illuminate the mind of Marowitz than that of Hamlet, it was nonetheless challenging and fascinating. It caused critical and audience comment in a way that no routine production would have. That it was the American premier of this Marowitz invention also is indicative of the adventurous spirit of the Festival.

Outside, the Civic Auditorium is distinguished only by a large ceramic celebration of an American mythic hero, probably Johnny Appleseed. Inside, the auditorium itself is overlarge for drama—some 2,000 seats. With seven weekly performances, the mid-week average house is about 450, according to Carra, so a balcony curtain is used to make the house more intimate. Weekends see attendance rise to 600–700 spectators. For a very popular production, however, the curtain is opened to permit seating of 1,200–1,400 people. A 1971 staging of *Godspell* was so well received, for instance, that all 2,000 seats had to be available when it was performed. Tickets are inexpensive, and those students not using foundation subsidy programs are entitled to a 50 cent discount on their tickets. Senior citizens pay $1. Aside from the actual performances, there are not many Festival amenities or extras, in terms of the Morris Dancing and Renaissance Seminars which are so prominently featured at some festivals. Nonetheless, Lakewood is moving ahead in this area too. On Thursdays, Festival visitors can participate in a

series of eight buffet dinners. These have, as their high point, "Pre-Curtain Talks" by Shakespearean and/or theatre authorities, some of them from Cleveland, some from farther afield.

For its production, the Festival uses an apron added to the regular stage. At one time, a modified Elizabethan framework, based on the John Cranford Adams ideas of the Globe, was used. This has been replaced with a more flexible set of platforms, ramps, and steps which suggest no special period or place. Two fixed side-towers, which can be doorways or elements to anchor other set units to, still subtly manage to suggest the two side doors presumed to be a feature of the Elizabethan theatres. An astonishing number of variations can be played upon these units. For a *Richard III,* Warner Blake's sets evoked a vision of Pirenesi's famed collection of *Carceri,* the prison engravings, with their great brooding arches and ruined masonry. For *The Beggar's Opera,* which was in rep with it and three other plays, a few deft reshufflings of the basics, plus some cleverly designed panels and extras turned the same stage into an 18th Century London locale in short order. William French's cleverly conceived costumes, of course, are a very important component in such visualizations. From a technical standpoint, they are the "stars," ably supported by the sets and lights.

In addition to Carra's position, there are four important administrative jobs. There are about nine jobs for designers, production chiefs, and assistants, with a number of apprentices. Ushering, fund-raising, lobby sales, ticket promotion, public relations, window displays, costume catologuing and other useful activities are provided by community volunteers, making this Festival an interesting study in cooperation.

Los Angeles Free Shakespeare Festival

September was a rainy, chilly month in 1973. The Pilgrimage Theatre, beautifully carved out of a Hollywood hillside, was open to the elements. Not an encouraging beginning for a new Shakespeare Festival. But, during the four week September run, 20,000 people filled the 1,300-seat theatre. Gathered from all over the Los Angeles area, they came to see a modern dress version of *As You Like It* directed by Alfred Ryder. The company of 16 Equity actors and numerous apprentices was headed up by stars of the caliber of Penny Fuller, Kristofer Tabori, Roscoe Lee Brown, and Joan Van Ark. The Los Angeles Mime Troupe and Thee Right Pithee Players frolicked before the performances. Costume designer Joe Tompkins worked miracles with a small budget. Lighting designer Donald Harris created atmosphere with borrowed equipment. Russell Pyle was recruited from the Los Angeles Company Theatre to create the setting.

Los Angeles had all the marking for the perfect festival location. One out of 25 Americans lives in the Greater Los Angeles area. The cross section of races and levels of affluence are as diverse as in New York. Tourists continually stream through the area. Los Angeles has an unbeatable reservoir of professional acting and directing talent—even if their first allegiance is to television and films. As if to clinch the deal, the beautiful outdoor Pilgrimage Theatre has been sitting virtually empty since the 1960's when the Christians stopped performing their theatrical salvation of the pagans on a regular basis.

It looked like such a perfect festival location that producer Michael Dewell moved the National Repertory Theatre operations to the West Coast to found the Los Angeles Free Shakespeare Festival. It was not as easy as they anticipated, but the Festival's pilot season production, *As You Like It* did run during September of 1973—with the co-operation of the Los Angeles Department of Parks and Recreation and the American National Theatre and Acade-

The Pilgimage Theatre
Los Angeles, California 90028
(213) 469–3974
Artistic Director: Terence Scammell

120

my. The Festival's original plan for the first season had been to stage two plays, *Macbeth* and *As You Like It* over an eight week period. But Los Angeles, living up to its reputation, was not an easy town in which to break into show business. Lack of funding support forced the Festival to curtail the pilot season to one play for four weeks. Basically the tradition of live theatre is very new in the celluloid capital. In fact, until Gordon Davidson's Center Theatre Group began production at the Music Center's Mark Taper Forum in 1967, good professional resident theatre was an unfamiliar item in Los Angeles. It is a measure of the Free Shakespeare Festival's perseverance and dedication that they achieved a foothold in the Los Angeles community so quickly.

Founder-producer Michael Dewell's battle cry had been that "the Festival was to be a democratic theatre." In Los Angeles, democracy not only meant free tickets, on a first-come-first-serve basis, but it also meant free parking and free transportation from distant "poverty pockets." To support that first production, the Los Angeles County Department of Parks and Recreation rented the Festival the Pilgrimage Theatre for a nominal $1 a year, and provided office space, maintenance and support services. In addition, a prestigious committee of 1000 was set up to commemorate individuals who personally donated or helped secure $1000 contributions. The business community was solicited. If the Los Angeles Free Shakespeare Festival did not get started with the huge *Bang!* they expected, many in Los Angeles saw it as the beginning of, as Dan Sullivan of the Los Angeles Times noted, "a necessary tradition."

But, following up on their initial welcome was not as easy as the Festival and producer Dewell anticipated. Activities and planning during the winter of 1973–74 were far-reaching. The Department of Parks and Recreation was going to undertake some needed renovation of the Pilgrimage Theatre. A Free Public Theatre Foundation which included repre-

As You Like It

sentatives from the Mayor's Office, the City Council, the County, and the theatre community was formed. Funding was anticipated from both the city's and the Mayor's budgets. A summer season of three productions during a 12-week-run was planned, as well as the establishment of active apprentice and internship programs. Suddenly, however the young Los Angeles Free Shakespeare Festival found itself steering a perilous course through the politics of funding and personalities. They lost the Pilgrimage Theatre and various financial supports, and their exuberant plans for 1974 were reduced to a program of touring to Los Angeles City and County parks. In two mobile units, *Macbeth* and *Comedy of Errors* played four weeks each, to 28,000.

In preparation for summer 1975, Michael Dewell resigned from the Free Public Theatre Foundation— an umbrella organization under which the Festival had been operating. Peg Yorkin, much noted for her successful charity and fund raising work, was appointed president and executive director, and Terence Scammell, one of the original Founders, is the Shakespeare Festival's new artistic director.

With these administrative changes, the Festival is anticipating the return of financial support from public and private sources. They are once again planning enthusiastically. They will be returning to the Pilgrimage Theatre where they hope to produce a *Romeo and Juliet*. In addition, the Festival will tour a collection of scenes and sonnets, entitled *Shakespeare and His People,* to the parks. The Public Theatre Foundation also hopes to support mobile unit tours of Asian-American, Mexican-American, and Black theatre groups to the parks of the city.

These first several seasons have not been easy for the Shakespeare Festival—but the very fact that they are still in there fighting for Free Shakespeare seems to be a positive indication of a strong future.

The Pilgrimage Theatre stage *(above)* and aerial view *(right)*, home of the Los Angeles Free Shakespeare Festival

New Jersey Shakespeare Festival

Route 24 winds westward out of the over-industrial parts of New Jersey through quieter, green Revolutionary War towns before it reaches the campus of Drew University in Madison. On sticky-summer afternoons, the lush green campus is a shady oasis. People picnic under huge trees or attend Elizabethan banquets on Wednesday and Saturday; and as the sun sets, madrigal singers wander torch-lit campus walkways.

Drew University has been home to director Paul Barry's 11-year old, New Jersey Shakespeare Festival since 1972. The University's intimate, 238-seat theatre with raked audience seating and a small thrust stage, is a good base for the Festival, which has been enthusiastically received as a welcome addition to the cultural climate of Northern New Jersey. Paul Barry inaugurated his New Jersey Shakespeare Festival in 1963 at the Cape May Playhouse. They expanded to do three winter seasons in the Boston area, returning each summer to Cape May until the summer of 1968. Hot weather and no air conditioning resulted in poor box office receipts, and the Playhouse was demolished that Fall. The following two falls (1968–1969), the Festival toured the state, returning in the summer of 1970 to Cape May to perform in the ballroom of the Hotel Lafayette. After one season, that too was demolished. Throughout a homeless and theatreless 1971, negotiations were underway with Drew University where the New Jersey Shakespeare Festival opened in 1972.

For that season, the Festival assembled a cast of 13 Equity actors, 6 professional staff members, and 60 apprentices—all under the artistic direction of Paul Barry. During the 10 summer weeks, the company produced a women's lib *Taming of the Shrew, Troilus and Cressida, Beyond the Fringe, The Hostage,* and *The Bourgeois Gentleman.* They also ran a series of dance, drama, mime, and music programs on

Drew University,
Madison, New Jersey 07940
(201) 377–4487
June–November
Artistic Director: Paul Barry

Measure for Measure

Richard II *(below)*
The Taming of the Shrew *(bottom)*
Coriolanus *(right)*

As You Like It *(above)*
The Tempest *(right)*
The Taming of the Shrew *(far right)*

Monday evenings. When it was all over, the Festival had played to an 82.5 percent capacity and made a $41.31 profit on their $100,000 budget.

The 1973 season ran June 26 through September 9—one week longer than the previous year. Operating on the same $100,000 budget, Arthur Kopit's *Oh Dad, Poor Dad*, Tennessee Williams' *Summer and Smoke*, and John Osborne's *Luther* were staged in repertory with two Shakespeare works: *Coriolanus* and *As You Like It*. Barry's production of *Coriolanus* was set somewhere in the midst of World War II with the crowds dressed à la 1940's Italian. The Roman soldiers bore an amazing resemblance to General Patton and his American Army compatriots, while the invading Volscians storm-trooped around in Nazi uniforms. Resident set designer David Glenn's platform and step units doubled as Roman City street, enemy territory, and battlefields.

As You Like It moved that escapist romantic fantasy into the realm of bad King John, good King Richard, and Robin Hood all joining forces in Sherwood Forest. Court princesses were costumed in fairy tale medieval, while they made grimaces worthy of Cinderella's ugly stepsisters. Scenery design for this show required lengthy breaks to shift locales.

Once again the Festival ran a Monday night series of short plays, dance, and music programs. Children's Theatre matinees, apprentice workshops, adult workshops, and high school master classes continued as part of the summer. Programs in creative dramatics for ages 7–12, basic acting for ages 13–17, and production workshops for ages 13–17.

The 1973 season showed a 15 percent increase in subscriptions which filled just under 16,000 seats during the 11 week run. By 1974, subscriptions were up 46 percent—to 2,000 subscribers—and the audiences filled 20,000 seats. The 1974 company of 14 professional actors, 8 staff members, and interns from across the country presented two Shakespeare plays (*Measure for Measure, Richard II*) and three

Troilus and Cressida *(top)*
As You Like It *(above)*

others (*Steambath, Under Milkwood,* and *JB*)—plus the usual Monday night attractions. The budget was up to $120,000.

The New Jersey Festival is proud to point out that they are one of the few Equity companies to perform so much on so little. The budget is enthusiastically supported by community efforts of the Festival Guild which helps by selling subscriptions, organizing theatre benefits, theatre parties, and volunteering services wherever they can. A non-profit corporation, the Festival relies on deductable donations to meet costs. In 1972, donations totalled $31,171; in 1974, contributions stood at $32,000 from 27 corporations, 3 foundations, and numerous individuals—including the New Jersey State Council on the Arts, Allied Chemical Corporation, Beneficial Foundation, Ciba-Geigy Corporation, Merrill Lynch, Pierce, Fenner & Smith Foundation, New Jersey Bell Telephone, and Warner-Lambert Company. Contributions plus box office receipts of $92,000 put the Festival in the black.

But, the biggest dollar stretcher is the Festival's comprehensive and well-integrated apprentice program. Selected from over 1,000 applications, the 1973 apprentice company numbered 70 actors and technicians, ranging in age from 17 to 37. They came from 17 states and 47 colleges. The apprentices attend daily classes, act in supporting roles, understudy lead parts, produce apprentice workshops and the Children's Theatre productions. They also build scenery, costumes, and props. In other words, to get the very necessary experience, the apprentices do, for little or no money, what other Shakespeare festivals have to pay for. Nor is Paul Barry hesitant to admit that on their budget, they could not exist without the apprentice program.

Northern New Jersey residents and critics are strongly backing their new Shakespeare Festival, whose success in its new home looks assured. Local drama critic Betty Mount writes in *The Independent Press,* "By putting on the cream of the crop of classic and modern plays for the elite who appreciate, regional theatre will survive and flourish. We have a chance to be part of that flourishing elite by supporting this venture so close to home." Non-local critics have not always been so consistently enthusiastic in their praises; and some even tend to regard the Festival as "summer theatre"—thereby implying that they are not always subjecting the Festival to the same standards as they might apply to a year-round Equity Shakespeare company.

However, the New Jersey Shakespeare Festival is a serious professional company. Artistic director Paul Barry tries, each season, to look at the classics in some manner that might be meaningful to a contemporary audience. The director's interpretations may be questioned. The level of the acting, in the professional as well as the apprentice company, is not always even. Sometimes a costume design does not carry throughout the play. Other times, a set designer does not deal realistically with the limitations of the space. But these criticisms can be leveled at almost any company attempting a short summer repertory season. The fact is that the New Jersey Shakespeare Festival is trying—and frequently they succeed.

As a mark of their continually growing strength, in 1975, the New Jersey Shakespeare Festival will extend into a fall season at the Drew University campus. Three Shakespeare plays and two others will run in repertory from the end of June through the middle of September; and then a fall season of three plays will run from September through late November. The festival points out "an extended season is the realization of part of our long term goals—though we continue to work for larger budgets, and better salaries and eventually, we hope, a new, larger theatre."

Shakespeare at Winedale

University of Texas at Austin
Winedale Museum, Box 11
Roundtop, Texas 78954

August
Director: James B. Ayres

Summer weekends in August, visitors from all over come to Fayette County in South Central Texas. Their destination is Winedale Inn Properties, four miles East of Roundtop, eight miles South of Carmine which is halfway between Austin and Houston. Here, in this German area of Texas is a 130-acre site with eight restored 19th Century, Texas farm buildings—a stagecoach stop, two barns, an old kitchen and several houses, a collection of German American furniture, decorative arts and tools, as well as a cabinetmaker's shop. The property, now a part of the University of Texas system, was a gift from a former Texas governor's daughter, Ima Hogg, who intends it to be a research center for the folk life of German Texas.

Why the profusion of visitors in August? They have come to see the performances of Shakespeare that grow out of a summer session course taught by associate professor of English James B. Ayres of the University of Texas at Austin. The course (entitled "The Play: Reading, Criticism and Performance") has been meeting at Winedale since the summer of 1971. There, amongst the Eastern Red Cedar, the Post Oak, the Chinaberry, Catalpa, Pecan, and Mustang Grape from which Winedale gets its name, the students encounter the playwright through the medium of performance. It is Ayres' idea that the best way to study Shakespeare is not to read him, but perform him—a concept that developed as a result of his studies at Ohio State University under John Harold Wilson and Harold Walley, and from his work with the American Shakespeare Theatre.

This summer school in Shakespeare has grown from 11 students for two weeks in 1971 to its current six weeks of study for about 20 students. An integral part of the course has always been free public performance, even if (in the first years) it was only a collection of scenes from Shakespeare's various plays. The summer of 1973 saw their first full length production, *The Tempest*, staged on the last two weekends of the session. In 1974, the summer session was concluded with one weekend of scenes from *Othello, Hamlet, Macbeth, Henry IV,* and *Taming of the Shrew.* A full-length production of *Midsummer Night's Dream* followed on a second weekend, and later toured to Texas College at Tyler.

The plans for 1975 (which is Shakespeare at Winedale's fifth anniversary) include a performance schedule expanded to include three weekends. The play or plays to be performed during the session are not selected until the class meets and defines its summer project. While the students, so far, have been almost entirely from the University, Ayres will consider other interested students.

It must be remembered, however, that this summer session is in reality a function of the English department—not the Drama department—at the University. While the work is much admired by many audience members, Molly Ivins, who reported on the project for the Hogg Foundation noted that "in performance, which was never the primary goal, their Shakespeare is not the best ever produced, nor is it always good. But it is amazingly energetic and often marked by startling originality of characterization."

Director James Ayres frequently points out that it is the "Process not the product that concerns us at Winedale." And, that process is reminiscent of group encounter and ensemble acting experiments in the discovery of the meaning of a text. These are the kinds of warm-up exercises in text analysis that many professional theatre groups experiment with before they proceed to polish their understanding into professional productions. But, at Winedale, the understanding of the playwright through the perfor-

A Midsummer Night's Dream

Shakespeare seminar activities *(above and above right)* and pre-production ritual *(right)*

A Midsummer Night's Dream *(top and above)*

mance of his texts is the goal—not necessarily productions that hold up on a professional level. Although it is obvious that the summer sessions have produced works of merit—witness their tour.

This summer of experiencing the Bard extends beyond textual analysis and into production areas. Each student is responsible for the creation of his or her own costume—frequently a simplified medieval garment. They also design their own makeup, settings, and lights. All on an amazingly small budget—which in 1974 was about $8500 and in 1975 may climb to $9500. The lion's share of this money is, in actuality, spent on student room and board.

Ayres points out that Shakespeare at Winedale has never received any University or State support and all financing comes from foundations, business, and individuals. The current list includes: the Hogg Foundation for Mental Health, the Lemuel Scarbrough Foundation of Austin, William Hawn, Jr. (a former Winedale student), the Pearl Brewing Company, the Virginia Williams Scholarship Fund (established by past students in memory of a constant audience member), the Friends of Winedale (contributors to the Winedale Inn Properties) and individual donors who send money after visiting performances.

Those actual performances probably have more in common with the 19th Century history of Winedale than they do with 16th Century England. They take place in an exposed-beam barn and are surrounded by events like old fashioned stew suppers and concerts by the University's Collegium Musicum. As far removed from Shakespeare's Elizabethan, half-timbered theatre as this 19th Century Texas barn might seem, director Ayres says it has "all the virtues of Shakespeare's Globe: the bareness, the many levels, the dirt, and the simplicity of design."

Shakespeare Festival of Dallas

Declaring for Free Shakespeare, The Shakespeare Festival of Dallas, yet another band of intrepid Texans, has been devoting itself to staging Shakespeare plays for short July seasons since 1972. Under the stars at Dallas Fair Park (which also houses the former Margo Jones Theatre, the Museum of Fine Arts, and the Cotton Bowl), the Band Shell becomes backing for a Summer Stage which is built out from the shell to bring performances closer to the audience. The first summer, founder/producer Robert Glenn put on one performance of *An Evening of Shakespeare* for an estimated 2,000 people. In 1973, the festival grew to five performances of *Othello,* playing to just over 10,000; and in 1974, ten performances of two plays, *Taming of the Shrew* and *Romeo and Juliet* were staged for an audience of 20,000.

The Festival is still young, and without funding from the city fathers, but producer Glenn has already begun to hire Actors' Equity guest artists for the major roles. Productions make use of the Dallas design studios and university theatre talents. The 1974 setting, designed by George Pettit, was created from rental units including 16 platform and step units, and prefabricated units of three bridges, six banners, six curtains and maskings. The end result was a flexible series of levels that provide balconies and inner rooms in the Elizabethan tradition and adapt easily to all of Shakespeare's works. Costuming set the Festival a particular problem which was solved by an ingenious co-operation with the Southern Methodist University Theatre Department and designer Giva McBride. The costumes were rented from SMU, but half of the rental fee went for the

3525 Turtle Creek Boulevard
Dallas, Texas 75219
(214) 526–6021

July

Producer: Robert Glenn

Romeo and Juliet *(top and bottom)*

Othello

construction of new costumes that had been designed specifically for the Shakespeare Festival.

Producer Glenn's goals for the Dallas Shakespeare Festival are high. He points out that, "Shakespeare wrote vigorous theatre and we are attempting no less today. And it must be of professional caliber. I do not merely want free Shakespeare, I want major Shakespeare. And, this costs money." Already the work of the Dallas Festival has attracted financial support from local foundations like the Junior League, the 500 Inc., Dallas Shakespeare Club, the Owsley Foundation, and the Texas Commission on the Arts and Humanities. In addition they number several major corporations—including American Airlines and Sears—among their supporters. The Festival keeps local interest high throughout winter and spring by running a series of monthly radio shows and by presenting an educational program on the theatre and Shakespeare in schools, clubs, and recreation centers.

Local press reports of the productions are not yet consistently enthusiastic—but, nonetheless, they are supportive and encouraging about the group's potential. A potential which producer Glenn has expanded (along with the budget) each successive season. Projecting another two-play season for 1975 for more than ten performances, the budget is expected to run about $60,000—a far cry from their initial one performance season of $2,635. And, the Shakespeare Festival of Dallas is at work on a master five-year plan for their future seasons.

Fair Park Summer stage, home
of the Shakespeare Festival of
Dallas *(right top)* and crowd for
The Taming of the Shrew *(right)*

Shakespeare in Central Park

Each summer since 1962, the trees and greenery of a park in downtown Louisville have come alive with the activity of producing Shakespeare out-of-doors. For six weeks during July and August, three plays are staged on a Wednesday through Saturday schedule, for audiences numbering about 500–600 a night. Productions usually begin at 8:45 in the evening, thus simplifying the difficulties that many other festivals have encountered with lighting in the twilight hours.

It all began with a little theatre group, the Carriage House Players, who under director C. Douglas Ramey, were well-known in Louisville for their productions of Shaw and Strindberg—the kind of drama, as they put it, that "was not generally available in the area." In 1961, as part of a local arts festival, the Carriage House Players took an hour's worth of cuttings from Shakespeare into the park. The audience liked it. So did the company and the following year in conjunction with the head of the Department of Recreation, Ramey and his group put together a more ambitious program. The Department of Recreation gave them an old boxing ring and a circus wagon and they scheduled four plays the Carriage House had in repertory: *Othello, Macbeth, Julius Caesar,* and *Much Ado About Nothing.*

The following season, the city built a concrete stage for the group, now known as Shakespeare in Central Park, and using the Tanya Moiseiwitsch-Tyrone Guthrie-designed Stratford Ontario stage as a model, they constructed a plywood backing for entrances and multi-leveled staging.

Free Shakespeare in their Central Park is something that Louisville residents have come to expect, and over the years the audience has grown to include tourists travelling in the region. Douglas Ramey thinks that "the audience is wonderful and as close to Shakespeare's as you will find anywhere. Inner city residents, who have never seen plays before, sit

2828 Rockhaven
Louisville, Kentucky 40220
(502) 584–4946
July–August
Director: C. Douglas Ramey

The Taming of the Shrew *(top and above)*

side-by-side on blankets and part benches with well-travelled residents conversant in contemporary theatre." The Central Park Shakespeare has expanded into a sister organization, "Shakespeare for Schools," a project which tours the schools of Kentucky with the plays of Shakespeare.

What they have done, they have managed on modest budgets. That first summer Shakespeare in Central Park's budget was around $1000. Each summer, it has grown and averages about $15,000 for a six-week season. In 1974, when they staged *Midsummer Night's Dream, Cymbeline,* and *Hamlet* the budget hit $25,000—but that includes costs for replacing sound and lighting equipment.

Despite their deep roots within the Louisville community, Shakespeare in Central Park has, throughout its history, encountered trouble getting funding support. Each summer was a cliff-hanger to see if the city or state would come up with enough money to turn the private donations into another summer of productions. In other summers, termites or fires caused them to find donations of materials and labor to rebuild the stage backing at the last minute. However, the future for Louisville's Shakespeare festival now looks assured. The Metropolitan Parks and Recreation Board, which so many times in the past stepped in at the last minute, has finally made Shakespeare in Central Park a permanent item on its budget.

An indication of the impact they have made on Louisville occurred several seasons ago when Louisville's resident repertory company, The Actors Theatre, staged its first Shakespeare production. Producing director Jon Jory dedicated the production to Douglas Ramey and Shakespeare in Central Park noting, "we probably wouldn't be doing *Hamlet* tonight if Mr. Ramey hadn't helped build an audience for it."

Shakespeare Summer Festival

Neither mid-Summer's sweltering humidity nor our nation's capital crime problem can keep Washington residents and tourists from their July and August appointment with William Shakespeare. The outdoor Sylvan Theatre, on the South slope of the Washington Monument grounds, has served as the summer stage for producing director Ellie Chamberlain's projects since its first, 1961, season.

It is one of the many active urban festivals that combines entertainment on a long summer's evening with a chance to get out of city streets and into the greenery of a nearby park. But more than that, in the years since its inception, Washington's Shakespeare Summer Festival has established itself as a professional and creative force. All for free—through the kind auspices of the National Park Service, the District of Columbia Department of Recreation, and private tax-deductible contributions.

The Festival's past record, combined with the attractions of Washington itself, have made it possible for Ellie Chamberlain to gather a core of professional actors, directors, and designers for each summer's production. Directors from New York, guests from the Oregon Shakespearean Festival among others, work with a crew of acting faces familiar from Broadway, Off-Broadway, day-and-night-time television. Washington's relative proximity to New York has been a distinct advantage rather than any kind of cultural threat.

In fact, it was New York's own free Shakespeare Festival that inspired Chamberlain. After working one summer in Joseph Papp's then-infant project, she moved to the Washington area and saw that the city could benefit from such a summer entertainment. Washington may have the makings of a theatre town now, but until the Arena Theatre was established and the Kennedy Center built, Washington was always more interested in the drama of politics than the drama of plays.

1000 6th Street, S.W.,
Washington, D.C. 20024
(202) 393–3420
Producing Director: Ellie Chamberlain

The first summer season everything had a very amateur, community theatre feeling about it. Chamberlain talked the Capital Parks Division into letting her use the Sylvan Theatre which provides 1000–1200 seats and plenty of additional space to pull up a blanket. The Department of the Army lent trailers for dressing rooms. Volunteers painted sets and stitched costumes. Cab drivers and oriental language professors played parts. The costs came to $7,500. The Parks Division purchased $2,500 worth of lighting equipment. Textile manufacturers like Galey and Lord, and Crompton-Richmond donated fabrics; and private foundations donated funds.

By the second season the company hired some professional Equity actors. For the third year, the company turned Equity and ever since has been able to bill themselves as "Washington's only free professional theatre." They are currently operating on a special Equity contract which allows them to hire an unlimited number of extras. Until 1974 the Festival staged one production a summer, with the exception of 1962, when they performed both *The Taming of the Shrew* and *As You Like It*. By the 7th season's production of *Hamlet,* local newspaper critics, only tolerant until then, began to declare that the Festival had finally come of age.

The Shakespeare Summer Festival production list includes two musicals, *As You Like It* in 1969, and that now stock item *Your Own Thing* (based on *Twelfth Night*). In both 1970 and 1971, the Festival augmented Shakespeare with evenings of jazz, ballet, and music by the National Symphony and the Alvin Ailey American Dance Theatre. Finances forced them to drop these extra programs. In 1973, the acting company for *Othello* included Robert

The Sylvan Theatre, home of the Shakespeare Summer Festival, aerial view *(right top)*, and stage set for Troilus and Cressida *(right)*

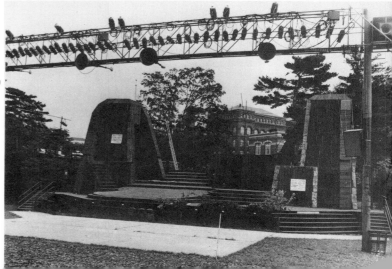

Troilus and Cressida *(above and right and facing page, left)*
Othello *(facing page, right)*

Guillaume (from *Purlie*), Tony Tanner (a familiar British face from *Half a Sixpence* and *No Sex Please, We're British*), and Cara Duff-MacCormack. The season, which was to run July 11 through August 12, proved so popular that the run was extended one week. As a further measure of the Festival's growth and acceptance in Washington and the surrounding communities, the 1974 summer production of *Twelfth Night* toured to four national parks before opening at the Sylvan Theatre, and during the last week of the season the company staged a second production, *The Importance of Being Earnest*.

Shakespeare Summer Festival productions usually begin at 8:30 p.m., which means that the first several scenes are played in twilight. A situation which has brought newspaper critics to comment on the budget quality settings until it is dark enough for theatrical lighting to set the tone, entirely. Designing costumes, sets and lighting for an outdoor stage

has never been easy. But when your theatre is at the foot of that overpowering monolith, dedicated to our first president, and within glance of the Capitol dome and Lincoln's columns, the problems of scale and impact are monumental.

Washington Post critic Richard Coe summed up part of the problem during the 1972 season, "If the setting provokes the imagination, it has its drawbacks, the latest being the disappearance of the huge tree which since its inauguration in 1919 had been the Sylvan Stage's chief glory and practical backdrop. Whatever the reasons, it's gone and the audience . . . now faces the lighted 19th Century windows of the Mint, where they make all that money that the Free Shakespeare Summer Festival hasn't got." Producer director Ellie Chamberlain is reluctant to discuss her current production budget but points out that it has varied up to $100,000 in their wealthy years.

In recent summers, scenic designers for the Festival have included Jack Doepp, Robert Yodice, and Richard Ferrer—each approaches the difficulties of creating a design that is not swallowed up by the surrounding architecture and environment in a different manner. Many outdoor theatres frequently find that the scale of costumes reinforces actor performance and presence, however the Shakespeare Summer Festival seems not to have explored this potential, yet. Some seasons they build costumes especially for their production and surroundings and in other seasons they rent costumes that were originally designed for another theatre's production.

While there has been talk about expanding the Summer Shakespeare to a longer, year-round schedule, producer Chamberlain hopes to tour to six area parks before opening in downtown Washington.

The Theatre
at Monmouth

Virtually all American Shakespeare Festivals prominently parade their dramatic wares by featuring the Bard's name in their titles. Not so Maine's interesting Monmouth festival. "The Theatre at Monmouth" is its proud name and no sub-headings referring to dramatic content are thought necessary.

Thus far, each season has four major productions, two or three of them being chosen from Shakespeare's works. The usual formula is two comedies, balanced by a tragedy or history play. Non-Shakespearean plays may also be classics, Dekker and Molière having been so honored, but there is no set rule about that. In 1972, there was an evening of Pinter plays, and, in 1974, George Bernard Shaw's *Caesar and Cleopatra* rounded out the bill. At special matinees, children's productions are offered. In 1973, James Thurber's *Thirteen Clocks* was popular with junior audiences, as was *The Sleeping Beauty* in 1974.

Apparently the reason Shakespeare's name doesn't get pride of place in the title is that the actual theatre is so lovely, so special, that the festival's founders, Robert Joyce and Richard Sewall, wanted *it* to get the honors. Shakespeare is already well known; he can stand on his own. But Cumston Hall and its theatre are unique in Maine, possibly even in America.

Cumston Hall contains an intimate recreation of a European Court Theatre. The architectural envelope is a large, handsome Victorian structure, complete with a stolid, square tower. Not only does the building contain a complete little theatre, but it also accommodates town meetings, local administrative offices, and the public library. Donated by Dr. Charles Cumston, the building was designed by Monmouth's own Renaissance Man, Harry Cochcrane. Obviously eclectic in his many talents, he saw no inconsistency in concealing his Court Theatre in an ornately carpentered 19th Century exterior.

Cumston Hall
Monmouth, Maine 04259
(207) 933–2952
June–September
Artistic Director: Earl McCarroll

144

The Festival's genesis, says one of its founders, teacher-playwright Richard Sewall, can be traced to his own love of the Theatre at Monmouth. In his youth, he had seen a Gilbert and Sullivan operetta there. Twice he tried to launch a Shakespeare festival alone, without backing or effective management. Only when he teamed with Robert Joyce, a drama professor from the University of Wisconsin at La Crosse, did he succeed. Initially, Joyce was also able to provide badly needed technical equipment and tools.

What is especially surprising and encouraging at Monmouth is the growth potential. Clearly, the summer season has its established limits, conditioned not only by the school year but also by the migration habits of tourists. The State of Maine, however, has a great many citizens who love theatre and want to enjoy it more often. Fall tours by the Theatre and a new Portland season show that there is an audience eager for a native live theatre. Artistic director McCarroll is so impressed by the response that he believes a year-round professional *classical* theatre operation could be sustained in Maine.

In 1974, following the Monmouth season, the professional players took two summer productions, *The Miser* and *The Taming of the Shrew* to the Portland Players' Thaxter Theatre for a mid-September engagement. As early as 1971, founder Sewall's condensation of *Richard II* and *Henry IV*, *The Royal Throne of Kings,* had been played to sixty-eight audiences from Kittery to Fort Kent in Maine. In 1972, Sewall and John Field, a mainstay of the ensemble, co-authored *Walt Whitman,* a one-man show. Field then toured this in Maine, following that with a national tour. The next venture for Sewall and Field has been *The Wooden "O",* a play dealing with one of Shakespeare's actors.

The Wooden "O" was also staged at Monmouth during the 1974 season, as part of a new Elizabethan

A Midsummer Night's Dream

Festival Week in mid-July. This event, inspired by similar festivities at Ashland and Stratford, proved so successful that it is to be regularly repeated. Among the highpoints: an Elizabethan banquet, with "cabaret" featuring scenes from Shakespeare's plays dealing with love and appropriately titled "The Food of Love"; Elizabethan music by the Monmouth Consort for a non-Elizabethan "downeast" clambake; Tony Montanaro's *Celebration Mime Theatre* on the green, followed by a barbeque; a crafts fair; a luncheon-fashion show of Elizabethan and modern clothes. Not only did these events make money; they also attracted attention to the theatre and the plays.

In its beginnings, Monmouth depended largely on college amateurs, high school students, and local enthusiasts for its casts, with a sprinkling of professionals. Fortunately, the enthusiasm dominated so that productions often had a sense of excitement which more than made up for an unevenness in skills and crafts of performance. Now, under the direction of Earl McCarroll, a drama professor at Ithaca College in New York, performance levels are higher and more uniform.

The Monmouth company operates under an Equity LORT D contract. It has featured as many as eight actors and actresses with Equity status and impressive professional credits. This is more than some larger festivals can boast. Among the acting apprentices, some are also asked to work on costumes and crew work where feasible. The Equity players get a standard wage. The apprentices are rewarded with room and board, plus a small weekly allowance.

This sense of community is everywhere evident at Monmouth. Actually, the visible community is not very large, so that the speeding tourist may have passed through Monmouth before he is aware that he is racing toward Augusta, Maine's capital city. As elsewhere, this festival depends heavily upon the volunteer work of local teen-agers and older citizens for such chores as ushering, car-parking, program-selling, and refreshment-vending.

Special praise is deserved by the Monmouth Women's Committee. Actually, it has members from all over Maine. The Elizabethan Week is its major project to raise money to offset the theatre's deficit. Outside the festival season, such events as bake sales and a two-day antique show also raise needed funds. There is an annual Elizabethan Evening in the Blaine House, with the Governor and his lady as the host and hostess. At this social event, cast members in period costumes mingle with theatre patrons and potential donors.

"Grass-roots" support is fundamental to the current success and continuing survival of most of the Shakespeare festivals. But, since the Theatre at Monmouth and its out-of-season activities will always be deficit operations, more dependable, fixed subsidies are needed from state and federal sources. The Maine Commission on the Arts and Humanities does help—as does the nearby Augusta AAUW, the Bank of Maine, and many business and private patrons. The National Endowment for the Arts has given $10,000, $6,000 of it earmarked for the fall touring. McCarroll and his trustees know that the Festival's impressive growth and improvement in quality make it an attractive candidate for such support. In the 1974 season, he notes, houses were generally sold out, and all past debts were paid off. With inflation, however, grants are essential to sustain the quality and continuity of the work.

Monmouth's tiny theatre—349 seats, only 300 of them with really good sight-lines—prohibits increasing revenues by attracting larger audiences. Its intimacy also includes the stage area, so "Less Is More" is an artistic guideline. Fortunately, Shakespeare's works do not require acres of scenery or tons of mechanical gimmicks. With a slim budget, a

Cumston Hall, home of the Theatre at Monmouth

148   The Theatre at Monmouth

tiny stage, and a small ensemble, less simply *has* to be more. It is not a matter of choice. Designers such as Vittoria Cappecce, Burton Bell, Fran Brassard, and Paul Gallo have learned how to achieve effect and economy in sets, costumes, and lighting. Cleanness of line, spareness of decor are essential for such a small space. Visual accents are provided by colorful costumes, props, and lights.

The proscenium opening of the Cumston Hall stage is 17' by 19', and behind this frame the stage is only 10' deep. If that doesn't seem cramped, consider the fact that there is no overhead space to fly scenery—and virtually no wing space. On the sides, the area available is about a quarter of a circle with a 10' radius. There are stairs leading to forestage boxes on each side, and doors leading to the lower level of the forestage. Stage left, there is a narrow stairway leading down to improvised dressing rooms below. To cross behind the scenes, actors have to walk outside the building on a semi-enclosed balcony. Formerly, the only way to make such a cross was to get on a platform under the stage and be wheeled across.

Fortunately, in 1973, the acting space was enlarged by building a new staging area, incorporating the gradual forestage extensions of previous seasons. Burton Bell, a costume designer, says, "We hope to evolve a basic stage which can be changed with plugs, steps, and ramps to suit the needs of any production." Obviously, any increase in stage space cuts down auditorium seating, though it doesn't affect the balcony.

For 1975, the Theatre at Monmouth's bill is *The Tempest, King Lear, The Comedy of Errors,* and a Shaw double-header: *Androcles and the Lion* and *The Dark Lady of the Sonnets.* As in three previous seasons, Professor Robert Hapgood, of the University of New Hampshire, will conduct a three-week Shakespeare Workshop. This is associated with the Festival and based at Maine's Bowdoin College.

The Throne of Kings, a condensation of Richard II and Henry IV *(facing page, top left),* Julius Caesar *(facing page, bottom left and top right),* Much Ado About Nothing *(facing page, bottom right)* and the European Court Theatre at Cumston Hall before the 1973 renovations *(above)*

Utah Shakespearean Festival

Adams Memorial Theatre
Southern Utah State College
Cedar City, Utah 84720
(801) 586–9061

July–August

Producing Director: Fred C. Adams

What is only a short trip from Zion National Park? From Bryce Canyon National Park? From Grand Canyon National Park? Not to mention from Cedar Breaks National Monument, Glen Canyon Dam, and Lake Powell?

All these magnificent, monumental wonders of nature—with some help from man in Glen Canyon—are located near a tiny Southern Utah town called Cedar City. Or, if you want to focus on Cedar City's major summer tourist attraction instead of the town itself, Grand Canyon and Zion Park are not far from the Utah Shakespearean Festival! As soon as the dedicated Shakespeare student or the determined theatre critic has secured his play tickets and his motel room, he is likely to plan excursions to Zion and Bryce, not wanting to miss the remarkable double-bill of geological theatre by day and Shakespearean theatre by night.

Fred C. Adams, producing director of the Cedar City Shakespeare performances, notes that things were once the other way around. If anyone stopped over, it was because he wanted a central base from which to explore the wonders of the area. "But," he asks, "*what* do you do in a Utah park after the sun goes down?"

The idea of a summer drama festival seemed a logical answer. Adams and a colleague, Douglas Cook, decided Shakespeare should be the festive focus. Before launching Utah's homage to the Bard, Adams toured all the major Shakespeare festivals to learn what he could from their failures and triumphs. Then in 1961, Southern Utah had its first Shakespeare fest. The Festival may import most of its able professional staff and its largely youthful acting company, but visitors to Cedar City have the immediate sensation of being guests at a home-town affair. The foyers and exhibit rooms of the college

Macbeth

auditorium are always crammed with attractive displays of costumes, props, and Shakespeareana—some of it possibly on loan from the Folger Shakespeare Library in Washington, D.C.

In the late afternoons on performance days, visitors work their way through the exhibits into a park area protected by the auditorium. There, to the left of the indoor theatre, is a handsome yellow-panelled and brown-shingled evocation of an Elizabethan theatre. It is an attempt to suggest the Globe Theatre and its staging areas. But, for several good reasons, it bears the name of "The Adams Memorial Theatre," and not that of the Globe. In its vicinity are a puppet-theatre—with Elizabethan decor, a Tudor musicians' pavilion, a dancing-floor for pre-performance period dance exhibitions, and several concession stalls.

The women of Cedar City, sweltering under the hot afternoon sun in their heavy Elizabethan costumes, serve oranges, fresh baked fruit tarts, and horehound candy, made from a 400-year-old recipe. They also usher the audience to their seats.

In 1974, the hexagonal open-air theatre complex was completed with the addition of some 740 permanent seats, in pit, loge, and balcony. And more seats can be set up on two promenade levels, one running behind the lower seats and one behind the balcony level. No seat is more than nine rows, or twenty feet, from the large thrust stage, with its inner and upper acting areas.

Max Anderson, a member of the Utah State Building Board, has drafted Cedar City's charming theatre

Adams Memorial Theatre,
home of the Utah Shakespearean Festival, on stage:
Much Ado About Nothing *(left)*
King Lear *(near right)*
The Comedy of Errors *(center)*
Macbeth *(far right)*

project from design suggestions of Douglas Cook, associate producer of the Festival.

The theatre has not been christened the Cedar City Globe, partly because Adams and Cook are well aware of the limited information available on that historic playhouse. In naming it the Adams Memorial, however, the Festival management honors a pioneer theatrical family who first brought a love of Shakespeare and the drama to Southern Utah settlers. The Mormons, unlike the Protestant Fundamentalists, always encouraged the cultivation and enjoyment of theatre and other performing arts. The old Adams stock company, with such dedicated players as Thomas, Will, and Luella R. Adams, helped theatre take a firm root in the salty sands of Utah. Today their memory is celebrated in the Cedar City theatre, made possible by grants from Grace Adams Tanner and her husband, from the Eggertsen Foundation, and from many Festival friends.

A 16th Century London street is being recreated along the college auditorium wall. An Elizabethan Knot Garden is to enhance the atmosphere. Other period amenities will be added to summon up echoes of an English past on the Southern Utah State College campus.

Usually, the Festival program offers three Shakespearean plays, often two comedies and one tragedy. Professor Adams always directs one of them. In recent seasons, a young actor-director, Richard Pilcher, has also proved himself, notably with a *Comedy of Errors* that was bright, fresh, and funny.

Fred Adams staged *Henry VIII* for the 1974 season, supported by Burt Peachy, who directed *As You Like It,* and Michael Finlayson, who mounted *Hamlet.*

The acting company is assembled by auditioning graduate students in theatre from the nation's best training schools. Among these, according to Adams, are: Baylor, Tulane, Yale, Stanford, UCLA, Santa Barbara, Brandeis, and Penn State.

In addition to their performance schedule, the

players are often required to run daytime rehearsals. There are also regular morning and afternoon classes in movement, diction, interpretation, and improvisation, so the company is continuing its technical training, both by precept and by practice.

For the season of nearly nine weeks, each actor or technician receives a stipend of $150, plus board and room. The accommodations are clean and attractive; the food, wholesome and plentiful. The scholarships which make this actor-support possible come from Scholarship Donors, members of the Festival Guild, local merchants, and from Cedar City itself. The summer maintenance cost, per player, is about $560.

The annual budget for the Festival is just over $50,000. "It's a pittance," says Adams, "but don't knock it. It has taken me years to get it up to that." Some $30,000 comes from box-office receipts, with $4,000 from such concessions as the fruit tarts and horehound candy. There are also major grants from the Utah State Institute of Fine Arts, the National Endowment for the Arts, and several private foundations. Avon Products and U. S. Steel have contributed. Not included in the total budget are such essentials as the buildings, services, and utilities provided free by the college; the time and effort contributed by Cedar City citizens, and donated goods and services from the region and the state. The producers of Arden Gold and Meadow Gold milk, for instance, give the Festival free air time on their commercials and even print large Shakespeare ads on the panels of their milk cartons all summer. This carries the news of Cedar City Shakespeare up into Idaho and down into Arizona.

What's more, it helps attract an audience which is now coming from all over the American West. And they are coming specifically for Shakespeare, not for the national parks. "That's just something to do during the day," Adams insists. "They want their Shakespeare—the parks are secondary.!"

A Midsummer Night's Dream *(facing page)*
In the dressing room *(above)*

Shakespeare Tours

National Shakespeare Company

In the years since 1963, artistic director Philip Meister and managing director Elaine Sulka have turned a $15 investment into a professional, classic repertory, touring company, which in its turn has given birth to an experimental program in dance, poetry, film and drama, a second touring company specializing in musicals, and a summer conservatory intent on training the pre-professional actor.

The National Shakespeare Company came into being when Meister and Sulka turned their $15 fee for a program of excerpts from great pieces of dramatic literature into a six-week tour of Shakespeare's plays to schools. By the second and third season, the company was touring 26 weeks, coast to coast, and they currently find themselves in a bus touring nine months a year, taking plays from New York to California, from Pocatello, Idaho, and over the border to the Western Manitoba Centennial Auditorium. Along the way the National Shakespeare has grown away from high school bookings and now plays almost exclusively in the university and college circuit. Since 1967, as their market began to demand more, the National Shakespeare Company branched out to include other "classic" playwrights in their repertory. Typical touring programs have included in 1972, *Midsummer Night's Dream*, *King Lear*, and *Antigone*; in 1973–74, *Saint Joan*, *As You Like It*, and *Julius Caesar*; in 1974–75, *Two Gentlemen of Verona*, *Merchant of Venice*, and *The Miser*. Plans for 1975–76 are to tour *Macbeth*, *The Tempest*, and *Much Ado About Nothing*.

Artistic director Meister sums up the company's approach to Shakespeare saying, "we start with the premise that the audience must understand the play. The Elizabethan language sometimes poses a barrier, but we can compensate for that by the stage action. We insist on playing our Shakespeare straight." In addition to Meister himself, the team of directors who have worked wth the National Shakespeare

414 West 51st Street
New York, New York 10019
(212) 265–1340
Artistic Director: Philip Meister

Company has included names like John Houseman, Gene Frankel, Maurice Edwards, David Baumberger, and Louis Criss. In early seasons, the Company frequently toured on a League of Resident Theatres contract, which they have since replaced with a letter contract. They no longer cast entirely in New York, and the Company feels that the national auditions have brought in many young, talented actors who are not yet members of Actors Equity. As part of their touring program, the NSC has also been in residence at Princeton University and the University of Massachusetts.

In 1968, the Company moved into its current headquarters which also house offices, costume and scenic shops, rehearsal studios and storage space, in addition to an intimate theatre, the Cubiculo, which has concentrated on experimental arts programs in poetry, dance, films, and drama.

In 1973, the National Shakespeare began to branch out in still more ways. Not content to tour Shakespeare for nine months of the year, they established a summer residency in Woodstock, New York. Their initial idea was to produce not only their own work but to bring in other companies—extending the work of the Cubiculo. The professed goal was to create a Cultural Arts Center in Woodstock. However, the playhouse which had been their base was sold to another producer and the NSC moved into a neighboring arts colony where in 1974, they sponsored their first 8-week summer conservatory. Studies for approximately 18, pre-professional students included acting style, script analysis, performance speech, voice production, mime, movement, tumbling, and playwriting for the actor. For their second summer in 1975, the Conservatory expects between 22 and 30 students.

Growing out of the Woodstock experience as well as the company's continuing attempts to reach beyond Shakespeare was the creation, in early 1975,

The Two Gentlemen of Verona

A Midsummer Night's Dream

King Lear

160 National Shakespeare Company

The Two Gentlemen of Verona

The Two Gentlemen of Verona *(left)*
The Merchant of Venice *(left bottom and below)*

162   National Shakespeare Company

The Merchant of Venice

of a second touring company. Not a repertory of Shakespeare and other classics, but one of full length musicals staged for performance in small auditoriums and coffee houses. The New York Theatre Company's first season included *Apple Tree, Fantastiks,* and *Berlin to Broadway,* and the second season is scheduled for *The Fantastiks* and a musical version of *Spoon River Anthology.*

Like many other theatre groups in North America, Philip Meister and the National Shakespeare Company have found that, combined with modern day talent, Shakespeare can be a very good stepping stone. In this case, Shakespeare led to the creation of an experimental arts center and conservatory training program, and a company touring musicals.

According to the company's general manager, Albert Schuman, the National Shakespeare fills a very specific need—one not covered by any other theatre company, because they are the closest thing we have to an old-fashioned touring company. Their specialty is that they are equipped to stage one-night stands in colleges and universities far from the regular touring, bus and truck circuits. Nor are they touring with the purely minimal sets and costumes that many touring companies would be tempted to do. Each season costume and set designers put together carefully designed shows which tour on a self-contained unit set. This unit set, designed by Meister and Karl Eigsti, builds up from the floor creating a raked stage from sectioned aluminum grating, and erects a grid and lighting overhead in little over an hour. This enables the company to put on a production in the simplest gymnasium or the most perfect proscenium theatre—and each production has the same consistently professional quality.

New Jersey Shakespeare Festival of Woodbridge

Simple, unpretentious and with no practical ambitions to be anything other than what they are—that is the Shakespeare Festival of Woodbridge, New Jersey. Do not confuse them with the very active and professional Shakespeare Festival at Drew University in Madison, New Jersey. The Woodbridge group is almost single-handedly the work of producer Rose Belafsky—housewife, mother and grandmother—she babies the Festival along out of sheer love of the theatre.

In the summer of 1961, Belafsky managed to talk the Woodbridge Township into supporting a Shakespeare Festival; and ever since the group has been a project of the Department of Recreation. They provide free theatre for the town and are invited to do the same in several surrounding communities. Funds are requisitioned from the Department of Recreation to pay the one salaried post—that of director—and to pay for costume and prop materials. The annual budget is in the $3,000 range. All the labor is volunteered by handy-with-a-needle housewives, clever-with-a-hammer-and-saw businessmen, or electrically-inclined students.

The acting company is recruited from local little theatres. Formerly aspiring actors and actresses who, for either money or marriage gave up their professional status, are also available. The group is considering applying for Equity showcase status to permit Equity "guest" performers. Although there seems little likelihood that Equity guests could be paid, unless the Woodbridge Festival applies for and receives a grant from the National Endowment for the Arts to encourage their expansion into In-School production during the academic year.

The Festival sets up annually for a short summer run in Woodbridge, and nearby town playgrounds and parks. Bleachers are arranged on three sides of a grassy plot which serves as a stage. Simple, freestanding props and scenery complete the stage.

428 South Park Drive
Woodbridge, New Jersey 07095
Producer: Rose Belafsky

Lighting controls and dressing rooms are housed in a nearby mobile unit.

The Woodbridge Shakespeare Festival's perseverance in the face of local apathy is amazing. Situated in a New Jersey no-man's-land, surrounded by smelly factories and impersonal oil companies, the audience response has not been encouraging. However, producer Belafsky points out that in the last four to five years there has been a shift in local population, bringing more theatre-going residents into the area. Prospective audience members have even been turned away in the last two seasons. In the Festival's first (1961) season, they played six performances for an audience of 2,500. By 1972, they had grown to 12 performances for an audience of 10,000. In 1973, a young, former company actor—turned director, Ron Davids, pulled the group into shape for a well-received, modern dress *Comedy of Errors;* and he returned for the 1974 season to stage a traditional *Two Gentlemen of Verona.*

The New Jersey Shakespeare Festival of Woodbridge is a non-professional, small community theatre effort. They are happy with their present status, and according to producer Rose Belafsky, have very little ambition to change the status quo. With a bigger season and a bigger company come bigger problems. But, in the meantime, they are providing an informal theatre experience for many New Jersey residents whose exposure to Shakespeare might otherwise be confined to high school assignments of *Macbeth* and *Hamlet.*

Twelfth Night *(right top)*
The Comedy of Errors *(right)*

New Shakespeare Company

Asked what is *new* about their New Shakespeare Company, the husband-producer and wife-director team of Roma and Ricklefs have a simple, direct explanation. In fact, simplicity and directness, they believe, are distinctive features of their approach to Shakespeare. No bizarre Peter Brook visions nor avant-garde gimmicks confuse their productions.

"We try to make Shakespeare new in the sense of going back to the way it was done four hundred years ago," says Ricklefs. He agrees that there is much that cannot be known with certainty about Elizabethan acting and staging, but the New Shakespeare troupe is trying to work with bare essentials—a stage with varied acting areas, virtually no settings, colorful costumes, and, of course, the Master's texts. "It's simpler to stage Shakespeare this way," he insists. "We want to get back to what Shakespeare was really saying. Of course he was a great poet, but he was a poet only incidentally. First, he was a playwright and a story-teller. And *that*, his genius as a playwright, is what is important."

As proof of the validity of their approach, Ricklefs and Roma point to their annually increasing success over the past four years on the college circuit, to the fact that they are a year-round operation, and to the encouraging statistic that they are able to give employment to a troupe of some 28 theatre people.

The New Shakespeare Company is professional, Ricklefs insists, but he admits that it is not Equity. The professionalism results from the thorough training ensemble members have received from Ms. Roma—author of *Acting in Our Time*—in workshops, rehearsals, and on the road. Given the fees paid by colleges, the basic operating expenses, and the size of the company, salaries work out to about $200 to $400 a month, depending on the degree of skill and amount of work contributed by the individual player. In addition, travel and living expenses, as well as insurance and other benefits are

*1668 Bush Street,
San Francisco, CA 94109
(415) 771–5290*

*Director: Margrit Roma
Producer: Clarence Ricklefs*

166

borne by the company management.

During the 1974–75 college season, the New Shakespeare toured with productions of *Hamlet, The Merchant of Venice, As You Like it,* and *A Midsummer Night's Dream.* Four station wagons and a truck keep the company mobile. An effective and flexible system of platforms, ramps, and stairs, designed by Ricklefs, packs easily into the truck, along with costumes and lighting equipment.

Current fees are: one performance—$2,250; additional performance on the same day—$1,400; additional performance on following day—$1,700, and a two-hour workshop conducted by Ms. Roma—$500. No union affiliations are involved. The troupe travels with 20–23 performers, three technicians, and the director herself. Motel accommodations are always used.

There is a fall tour of about two and a half months through colleges in the Northeast, South, and Southwest. During the winter months, the troupe is primarily at its home-base in San Francisco's Trinity Episcopal Church, but it is constantly making short performance trips to Pacific Coast colleges. In spring, further performances are given on the college circuit on the West Coast, in the Southwest and South, and also in the Midwest and Great Lakes.

Ricklefs believes that the New Shakespeare has made impressive inroads on the territory of other touring Shakespeare groups. The troupe's publicity kits include enthusiastic testimonials from such varied schools as the University of California at Los Angeles (UCLA), Hobart College, University of Massachusetts, Vanderbilt University, and William and Mary. Other well known institutions which have engaged the New Shakespeare players are Goucher College, Miami University, Oberlin College, Sweet Briar College, Butler University, University of Illinois at Urbana, University of Nebraska, Lewis and Clark College, and San Jose State.

The Merchant of Venice *(top)*
A Midsummer Night's Dream *(below)*

The Merchant of Venice *(top)*
As You Like It *(left)*
A Midsummer Night's
Dream *(below)*

Productions can be staged with equal ease indoors or out; in theatres, gymnasiums, or ballrooms. Because of the compactness of the troupe, the New Shakespeare prefers to have each sponsor provide the stage crew and the lighting. There are extra fees, if the troupe has to provide its own lighting.

The lighting designs of Peter Belohlavek and Connie West's costumes are often singled out for praise by college reviewers.

The recent success of the New Shakespeare Company is the realization of a long-held dream of Margrit Roma. As a young actress, the Zurich-born theatre woman worked in Berlin with Bertolt Brecht and Erwin Piscator. She also was exposed to the training of Max Reinhardt. When the Nazis came to power, she fled to Paris, then to the Los Angeles area. There she tried to establish a permanent theatre ensemble, but she found that neither audiences nor actors could be depended upon, owing to the way of life.

Coming to San Francisco, she and her husband/colleague Clarence Ricklefs made a new start. He at first helped support the operation through school-teaching as well as producing. Actually, the local experiment began in 1965 in the Palo Alto area, south of San Francisco. In 1966, Roma and Ricklefs moved to San Francisco. In 1967, they mounted their first production. In the 1968–69 season, they tried to find a solid footing for the New Shakespeare as a kind of little theatre operation. Unfortunately, as so many other dedicated groups have found, San Francisco is really not all that much of a theatre town. And the attractive 90-seat theatre they created in Trinity Episcopal was also too small to be economically viable—though it is excellent for rehearsal work.

Realizing that they couldn't play solely in their church-theatre, they began touring, initially among the many schools and colleges in and around the Bay Area. Spring weekend afternoons, the troupe played in Golden Gate Park. In summers they appeared at

Armstrong State Park and other locales. Currently, summers are spent at Lake Tahoe, both on the south shore and the north shore. At the northern end, a special outdoor theatre has been built for them. In January 1975, the New Shakespeare did give San Francisco a four-weekend season of its repertory. With the apparent demise of the Marin/San Francisco Shakespearean Festival in the summer of 1974, the company replaced them at the San Francisco Palace of Fine Arts for a June–July season.

Ultimately, Roma and Ricklefs would like to have both a touring company and a company resident in San Francisco—rehearsing and performing. And a training company to fill vacancies in the two ensembles. At present, as many as five students from Ms. Roma's workshops will move into the company each year. As new players join, older ones move on to other theatre work, but there is always a young, experienced corps to provide continuity.

In 1970, the New Shakespeare received a one time grant of $20,000 to enable Ms. Roma to conduct an on-going workshop for 18–20 students, many of them from underprivileged backgrounds, and with emphasis on performance in neighborhoods. The funds also helped pay salaries for the first few months of those invited to join the ensemble.

In 1968, the company began to receive support from a special San Francisco city fund, raised from the hotel tax. William Ball's famed ACT—the American Conservatory Theatre—also is partly supported by this subsidy. This fund, designed to help advertise and publicize San Francisco, has aided the New Shakespeare because its work is making the City by the Golden Gate better known around the nation, as well as enriching the city's cultural life when the troupe is not on the road. $15,000 is a typical annual grant. The Trinity Episcopal Church office and rehearsal spaces are of course also a valuable subsidy, for which the congregation and its pastor, the Rev. Hugh L. Weaver, are responsible.

As You Like It

Southeastern Shakespeare Company

Box 1215
Henderson, North Carolina 27536
(919) 492–2078

Producer/Managing Director:
Charles M. Smith

The Southeastern Shakespeare Company could aptly be described as an "intrepid band of travelling players." Touring with the support of the North Carolina Department of Public Instruction, the Southeastern Shakespeare Company is dedicated to introducing "Shakespeare to young people so they will enjoy it and not fear it." And this they do throughout the school year at high schools, junior colleges, and colleges in the region.

Southeastern Shakespeare is the dream and creation of one man—Charles Smith—and it is through his continued dedicated and energetic efforts that the company gets funding, housing (on a 70-acre farm), and bookings—which have increased each year since the troupe's establishment in 1972. Charles Smith started out to be a college soccer coach, which he did successfully for a number of seasons. But the smell of greasepaint that he encountered acting in the area's outdoor historical dramas proved too strong. He went back to college for an M.A. in drama; his thesis was the organization of a Southeastern Shakespeare Company. He proceeded to do just that in the fall of 1972.

The company's main thrust is educational; the creation of superlative theatrical experiences comes second to the teaching aspect of their work. They tour a program called *Shades of Shakespeare* which Managing Director Charles Smith says he "wrote" himself. What he actually did was to write a narration that ties together scenes from various Shakespeare plays. High school level audiences can choose between two, 60-minute programs: one contains scenes from *Romeo and Juliet, Taming of the Shrew,* and *Macbeth;* the second series features *Julius Caesar, Taming of the Shrew,* and *Othello.* For college level audiences, a 100-minute program includes scenes from all five plays. According to Smith, "the plays selected for the program are those frequently studied in English classes and the select-

Shades of Shakespeare: scene from
The Taming of the Shrew

Shades of Shakespeare: scene from Macbeth

ed scenes the most familiar ones. They contain lines often assigned for class memorization." In addition, the company does a workshop in Shakespearean dialogue entitled *Romeo and Juliet—Hee Haw Style.*

The company is non-Equity and composed of actors and actresses culled from regional auditions and university theatre training programs. Frequently, faces from the Southeastern Shakespeare Company show up on the stages of outdoor dramas during the summer. In order to facilitate touring, production values are kept to a bare minimum. Costumes are the simplest generalizations of a vague 16th Century period. Capes, cloaks, boots, daggers, and hats are added for emphasis on special roles. Settings are a few simple step units. The company notes that their show is "organized to be performed anywhere, with a minimum of lighting, without curtains, wings, or even a stage." Their primary concern is the dialogue written by Shakespeare.

Excerpting Shakespeare and performing selections of short scenes is the kind of work that makes Shakespeare scholars and purists, as well as many dedicated theatre-goers, cry out against "desecration of the Bard." Nonetheless, in their market, the Southeastern Shakespeare Company is enthusiastically received, and reviews in school and community newspapers are raves. Thus far, their reception has been good enough for Smith and his company to begin planning for expansion. Their hope is to build a theatre for rehearsals and year-round "stock" productions. Currently, they are working on adding a new show to their touring repertory—a full length *Street Car Named Desire.*

Shakespeare Celebrations

Hofstra
Shakespeare
Festival

For those who enjoy seeing Shakespeare's works on stage but who are only free to travel during summer vacations, the early spring scheduling of the Hofstra Shakespeare Festival may seem inconvenient. Some college festivals, like that of the University of Vermont, in Burlington, or of Southern Utah State College, in Cedar City, are designed to shape the skills of young performers while at the same time entertaining summer students and tourists alike. Hofstra's goals are broader, in education terms, and they require late winter or early spring performance dates. In 1974, the Hofstra Festival celebrated its quarter-century anniversary.

"One swallow doesn't make a summer," goes an old saying. In the formative years of the Hofstra Festival, this was amended by some cynics with the clause: "Nor does one play make a festival!" In recent years, however, the Shakespeare play chosen each year for major production has always been framed with a variety of Tudor, Elizabethan, and Jacobean entertainments, thoroughly justifying the festival epithet.

For Hofstra's 25th annual salute to the Bard, *A Midsummer Night's Dream* was the major production. Seven public and four school matinee performances were offered in mid-March. (Over half the cast of Hofstra's first *Dream* staging in 1963 have gone on to professional theatre work, underlining one of the goals involved in the Hofstra enterprise.) But *Dream* was hardly Hofstra's single swallow. David Amram's opera, *Twelfth Night,* with libretto by Joseph Papp—and probably Shakespeare, was also given full stage treatment. The First Chamber Dance Company provided a program including José Limon's *The Moor's Pavanne,* based on *Othello*

Hofstra University Playhouse
Hempstead, Long Island, New York 11550
(516) 560–3283

The Hofstra University Globe Theatre

This interesting, encouraging collaboration of college performing arts disciplines was also illustrated in a joint program of the Hofstra Collegium Musicum, featuring period music and songs, and the Hofstra Repertory Theatre, with a production of Shaw's one-act comedy about Shakespeare, *The Dark Lady of the Sonnets*. Festival offerings were rounded out with an international cinema series, showing Shakespeare's impact on contemporary drama, dance, and musical theatre, and an art exhibit, "Shakespeare and His World." 1975's centerpiece is *Love's Labour's Lost*. In the past, local high schools have used the setting of the major production to show scenes from Shakespeare's plays, after which their work has been critiqued by members of the drama faculty.

Perhaps the most fascinating aspect of the Hofstra adventure, at least for theatre scholars and Shakespeare specialists, is its "Globe Theatre." In fact, this presumed replica of Shakespeare's own theatre is intimately bound up in the reasons for founding a Festival at Hofstra. One of the strongest of the forces which have shaped Hofstra has been its president emeritus, Dr. John Cranford Adams. Dr. Adams, be-

fore he accepted leadership at Hofstra, had already earned for himself a reputation as a Shakespearean scholar. One of his most important areas of study was the nature of Shakespeare's stage and stagehouse. His researches made possible Dr. Adams' *The Globe Playhouse: Its Design and Equipment* (1942). An outgrowth of this was the model of the Globe, as envisioned by Dr. Adams, which is now on permanent display in the Folger Shakespeare Library in Washington, D.C. Dr. Adams was assisted in constructing the one-twelfth scale model by Irwin Smith. Later, Smith also wrote a book on the subject: *Shakespeare's Globe Playhouse: A Modern Reconstruction* (1956).

When the Hofstra Festival was inaugurated, its present site, the handsome, lavish Playhouse did not exist. A gymnasium, which did duty for a variety of educational and leisure activities, had to be transformed each spring into an evocation of Shakespeare's own stage.

The Hofstra Globe was based on Dr. Adams' designs, but some modifications had to be made for the gym—and more were made when the Globe stage

Richard III
*(facing page top, and
this page, top right)*
A Midsummer Night's
Dream *(this page, top left)*

was adapted for use as an inset in the Playhouse's proscenium aperture. Recalling those early Festival days, Dr. Adams comments: "The 'Globe Set' was originally designed for an improvised thrust stage in the gymnasium (hence its reduced height of 23 feet), where spectators sat on sharply rising bleachers placed on three sides. *Much* more effective—and accurate—than its transplant to the later Playhouse—where *all* spectators are in front and on average much lower down . . . The compromise was inescapable: *i.e.*, the 'Playhouse' had to serve a score of purposes; the gym could not each year be taken from a sports and phys. ed. program and given over for 6–7 weeks to a drama binge! And oh! how comfortless the bleachers were, even with padding."

Questions of comfort did not deter student and Long Island audiences from patronizing and enjoying the early productions. Rapidly, the Festival became—and remains—an important college-subsidized cultural event in the area. Given the continuing guidance of President Adams, the Festival was also strengthened by the artistic direction of Dr. Bernard Beckerman, former head of Drama at Hofstra.

Considering Hofstra's preoccupation with the Globe Theatre, it is appropriate that Dr. Beckerman, while running the Festival, wrote *Shakespeare at the Globe* (1962).

Dr. Miriam Tulin has since become chairperson of the Drama Department and is responsible for the Festival's successful operation. She and her able staff are mindful of the varied goals of theatre activity in a liberal arts college: 1) as a very exciting introduction to the liberal arts, 2) as a vital, visible experience of human history and culture, 3) as a means to gaining increased self-awareness and ability to communicate with others, 4) as an initiation into the arts and crafts of professional theatre work, and, 5) as an opportunity to share earnest, enthusiastic student productions with the surrounding community, as an important public service.

Those goals may seem too diffuse to bring into focus; it is difficult enough just to get a play on—especially with teen-age amateurs—without having to think about such deep, long-term aims as well. Yet that is the mandate implicit in college theatre programs, and on the evidence of past practice, the Hof-

Richard III *(facing page)*
A Midsummer Night's
Dream *(top)*
Twelfth Night *(above)*

stra drama staff has been eager to meet that challenge. And meet it they do, with no sacrifice in production values for the general spectator.

One change Dr. Tulin has made is indicative of how both student-learning and audience-enjoyment are being served. Formerly, Hofstra, like so many colleges and universities, had an impressive program of major and studio productions, often as many as six major productions. Now much drama department work in the fall and winter is directed toward the Festival in general and the Shakespeare play in particular. There are other major productions and studio offerings but the really intensive study and most meaningful interpretive and technical work is concentrated on producing Shakespeare. Leading roles may be taken by professionals; the rest are played by students.

Under the guidance of talented set and costume designers, student actors and technicians build costumes and props, learning by doing. When budgets permit, every so often, the Globe stage will be replaced in the 1,134 seat Playhouse with a modern design. For *Richard III* in 1972, designer Richard Kramer combined some of the quality of Peter Brook's "Empty Space" with the devices of the Japanese Kabuki Theatre—notably a *Hanamichi,* or runway through the audience seating which enabled King Richard and his foes to make some impressive processional entrances and exits in the 75 lavish costumes Kramer and the students had so carefully made. When Globe is used, its various areas are dressed with flags, branches, thrones, and similar props which indicate location, period, and atmosphere. From the edge of the orchestra pit to the upstage curtain, its stage is 24 feet deep. When it is not in use, Professor Donald Swinney, Hofstra's technical director, has its parts neatly numbered and stowed away in the Playhouse, waiting for another in the long line of Hofstra's festivals.

Shakespeare at Columbus College

How does a small Georgia college get into the Shakespeare Festival business? In the case of Columbus College the answer is: almost by mistake. It all began in 1970 with the college's director of theatre, Dennis Ciesil, and designer/technical director, William Crowell. They started out to design a production of *The Taming of the Shrew*. They were looking for something spectacular to make an impression on the Southern Educational Theatre Conference, as well as to establish the infant Fine Arts Department as a vital force on the Columbus College campus.

Many cords of wood and 6,000 volunteer work hours later, they had constructed a three-quarter scale Globe Theatre. It took them four months from drawing board to completion and used up the Drama Department's budget for the year. From there, it was but a short step to involving the town and college in annual theatre department productions of Shakespeare during the winter quarter. Much like the Hofstra University Festival in New York, Columbus College confined its festive trimmings to the short run of their annual Shakespeare production.

Since the first *Taming of the Shrew*, Columbus College has also played *Richard III, Macbeth, The Merry Wives of Windsor*, and in March of 1975 *Henry IV*, on their portable Globe. The art department designs special tapestries. Weapons and armor are constructed with the help of a local blacksmith and the art department. The college theatre department, which has now grown to three full-time faculty, a part-time costumer, and 15 majors, spends a great deal of time recreating authentic costuming and props for their productions. Lectures of Elizabethan life, exhibits from the Folger Shakespeare Library, and occasional Elizabethan banquets, entertainments and games surround an evening's performance.

Each year local attendance at the festival in-

Columbus, Georgia 31907
(404) 568–2048
Director: Dennis Ciesil

The Columbus College Globe Theatre

The Merry Wives of
Windsor, in rehearsal
(below and bottom)

Forging armor *(right)*

creases. Beginning in 1974, the college incorporated their program with the local school system to bring in students from nearby. Their usual five performances were increased to eight and they played to a record 3500 people. Shakespeare at Columbus College has now come to a turning point. Their Globe Theatre is beginning to show signs of age and the college is facing a decision: To rebuild the Globe in stronger more durable materials or to abandon their Globe for a new staging concept—perhaps a commedia dell'arte wagon? Whichever way they decide Columbus College will continue to make Shakespeare a festive occasion for Georgia residents.

182 Shakespeare at Columbus College